Across the Plains
in Forty-nine

REUBEN COLE SHAW

The Lakeside Classics

Across the Plains
in Forty-nine

By
Reuben Cole Shaw

EDITED BY

MILO MILTON QUAIFE

CHICAGO

The Lakeside Press
R. R. DONNELLEY & SONS CO.
Christmas, 1948

Publishers' Preface

ONE hundred years ago, on January 24, 1848, gold was discovered in California. As the news of that discovery reached the Middle West and the states along the Atlantic Seaboard, fortune seekers started for the new El Dorado. Singly and in groups they went, by land and water, in ever increasing numbers and in 1849 the "gold rush" reached its height.

Much has been written to describe the trials and hardships of these adventurers. For this year's volume of The Lakeside Classics the publishers have selected one of these accounts, the narrative of Reuben Cole Shaw. While not as full of horrors as many of the accounts are, it tells of the difficulties of planning and carrying out an expedition through our then unsettled and little known western country and presents a vivid picture of its scenic grandeur.

The reader will get the most out of the narrative if he will read it against the compact background depicted by Milo Milton Quaife, the long-time editor of The Lakeside

ix

Publishers' Preface

Classics, in the excellent historical introduction appearing on pages xvii to xlv.

We are again indebted to the Newberry Library for its unfailing courtesy in giving us free access to its Ayer Collection which contains so much material not elsewhere or not otherwise readily available.

The year now closing has been a successful one for the company. The last unit of its plant expansion was completed during the first half of the year and, with the cooperation of the entire personnel, the organization was developed to take care of the increased activity. Major items of new equipment remaining on order are nearing completion and should all be installed and in operation by the end of the coming year.

Outside warehousing in Chicago will be consolidated in a building now being erected in close proximity to the plants, thereby adding the last step in the program begun immediately at the close of the war.

Once more we extend our best wishes for a Merry Christmas and a Happy New Year.

THE PUBLISHERS.

Christmas, 1948

Contents

xi

Contents

Contents

Historical Introduction

Historical Introduction

JOHN AUGUSTUS SUTTER had an astonishing career. A native of Baden, Germany, he acquired Swiss citizenship and served in the Swiss army. A born adventurer, he came to America in 1834 and before long was accompanying trading parties across the Plains from Missouri to Santa Fe.[1] In 1838 he went with a missionary party to Oregon, apparently with the intention of continuing from there to California. Unable to continue the journey overland, he set sail for Honolulu, and from there sailed to Sitka in Russian Alaska. The Russian-American Company then operating on the Pacific Northwest Coast had established trade relations with the Spanish settlements to the southward, and from Alaska Sutter succeeded in making his way to California in the early summer of 1839.

Evidently he had come with a plan of operations in mind, for within less than a week after his arrival at San Francisco Bay he ap-

[1] For the classic account of the Santa Fe trade see Josiah Gregg, *Commerce of the Prairies*, the Lakeside Classics volume for 1926.

plied to Governor Alvarado at Monterey for permission to establish a colony on the northerly frontier of Spanish settlement. His project won the Governor's approval and he was authorized to select a site, with the promise that the desired land grant would follow in due course of time.

The site selected for the colony was at the junction of the American and Sacramento rivers, and here in the summer of 1839, Sutter's employees began the arduous tasks of clearing land, plowing and planting it, and setting out orchards and vineyards. To serve as the seat of his principality, which he named New Helvetia, Sutter presently built a massive adobe walled fort which in reconstructed form can still be seen near the heart of Sacramento, California's capital city.

Favored by such beginnings, in 1841 Sutter was accorded Mexican citizenship, and along with this eleven square leagues of land for the development of his colony. So vigorously did he push the work that in 1845 an additional grant of twenty-two square leagues of land was awarded him. In his case, at least, the maxim that a rolling stone gathers no moss, was wholly inapplicable. Spanish California had never witnessed such an example of enterprise and energy as he afforded; and when the advance guard of

American settlers came drifting overland from the States, Sutter was in readiness to welcome and befriend them all.

By 1846 settlers were pressing westward across the intervening Great Plains in considerable numbers. In the spring of 1844 an ailing settler of northwestern Missouri, James W. Marshall, was advised by his physician to go West for his health. He joined a wagon train bound for California, but for some reason on reaching Fort Hall on the Snake he continued northwestward to Oregon.

From Oregon, in the following season he proceeded southward to California, arriving at Sutter's Fort on the Sacramento in July, 1845. Vicissitudes of fortune which we need not pause to recount followed. In 1847, once more penniless, Marshall entered into partnership with Sutter to construct and operate a sawmill, Sutter supplying the capital and Marshall the superintendence of the enterprise. The site selected for the mill was at Coloma on the south fork of the American, and here, on January 24, 1848, while engaged in deepening the tailrace of the mill, Marshall discovered some metallic flakes which proved to be gold.

Efforts to suppress the news of the discovery proved futile and soon San Francisco and the other California settlements were denuded of their able-bodied men, who abandoned their existing employments to engage in a mad scramble for gold.

The news of the discovery was carried eastward to the Atlantic Coast during the summer, and President Polk's annual message to Congress on December 6, 1848 touched off a wave of excitement which soon swept the entire country. The gold rush of 1849, whose centennial California is currently preparing to celebrate, followed. Thousands of hopeful fortune seekers went to California by sea, proceeding either around South America or across the Isthmus of Panama. Still other thousands, gathered alike from seaboard cities and from interior hamlets and farms, undertook to journey overland across mountains and plains to the new-found El Dorado, where, as they fondly anticipated, gold in ample quantities was to be had for the taking.

There were, of course, many overland routes and variations of routes, but the one followed by the largest number of gold-seekers was the famous Oregon-California Road. Its easterly terminus was some point on or near the Missouri River such as Independence, St. Joseph, Fort Leavenworth, or Council Bluffs. To these starting points settlers from widely separated points in the

Middle West or along the Atlantic Seaboard found their way, and presently all converged upon the Lower Platte River, up which and the North Platte they pursued their journey to the vicinity of Casper, Wyoming. Here they crossed to the eastward flowing Sweetwater, up which they continued to the famous South Pass of the Rockies in western Wyoming.

After crossing this well-nigh imperceptible backbone of the continent the main road turned southwardly to Fort Bridger, which afforded the first civilized stopping-point west of Fort Laramie. From Fort Bridger the road turned northwardly again to Fort Hall, near present-day Pocatello, Idaho.

At Fort Hall the Oregon Trail and the California Road separated. The former led on westwardly to and down the Columbia (Fort Hall was itself on the Snake or Lewis Fork of the Columbia); the California Road veered sharply southward to seek the headwaters of the St. Mary's or Humboldt River in northeastern Nevada, and descend this stream to the point where a crossing to the Carson was effected. Thence either by Carson River and Pass or by the Truckee River and Truckee or Donner Pass the Sierras were crossed, to debouch upon the mining area adjacent to the American and the Sacramento rivers.

There were, of course, important variations
in the route we have thus outlined, two or
three of which require present explanation.
At South Pass, instead of following the main
road via Fort Bridger to Fort Hall the emigrant might take the Greenwood, or Sublette, Cut-Off, which plunged directly westward across rivers and intervening desert to
rejoin the main road on the upper Bear in
southeastern Idaho. By the Cut-Off, a sav-
ing of several days' travel was effected, at
the cost, however, of crossing a considerable
stretch of desert, whereas the road by Fort
Bridger was well-watered.

Another and earlier variation of the route
from South Pass led northwardly into the
Wind River Mountains, and by a devious
trail impassable to wagons struck westwardly toward Fort Hall at some distance to the
north of the Sublette Cut-Off as already described. This route had been abandoned before the era of the Forty-niners, and but for
the fact that our author's party endeavored
to follow it, it would call for no notice here.

All three of the routes from South Pass re-
united on the upper Bear to run as one as far
as Soda Springs. Near here, however, still
many miles short of Fort Hall, in the summer
of 1849 was opened Hudspeth's or the Emigrants' Cut-Off, which ran southwestwardly

120 miles to a point on upper Raft River where it intersected the California Road coming from Fort Hall. Although the distance saved by the Hudspeth Cut-Off was comparatively slight, as soon as it was opened practically all emigrants bound for California forsook the older route in favor of the new Cut-Off.

Numerous variations in the route from Raft River to the Humboldt were followed. Once arrived on the Humboldt itself, still other choices were open to the emigrant. Probably the great majority continued down the river past Carson Sink and across to Carson River, to cross the Sierras by either the Truckee (Donner) or the Carson Pass. But many left the Humboldt at the Great Bend (vicinity of Winnemucca) to proceed thence westward across the desert and the intervening Sierras to northern California, whence they made their way southward to the upper Sacramento.

The dangerous and arduous character of the overland journey might well have reserved it for only young and vigorous men to attempt. Yet men already far gone in senility, as well as women and children of every age and degree of helplessness blithely entrained for California, either ignorant of or ignoring the obstacles and the dangers they must encounter. The fate of many was pitiful enough; especially pitiful was the lot of families whose head perished enroute, leaving a wife and helpless children to the mercies of the desert, to make their way onward or back as best they could; or, failing, to follow the husband in death.

The great majority of goldseekers, of course, won through, and so the Commonwealth of California was born. Many, too, won fame or fortune in satisfying amount. Yet often the roseate dreams of those who embarked upon the sunset trail were doomed to disappointment. So little was known in advance of the mining country, and so extravagant were the stories told in the East concerning it that resultant disappointment and failure for many were inevitable.

An argonaut who went by sea to California has supplied a vivid picture of the dreams which animated the goldseekers.[2] Many of the passengers spent their time on the voyage devising receptacles to hold the gold they expected to garner and there was hot argument over the respective merits of ale bottles and pouches made from boot legs, leading to eventual agreement that empty pork barrels which could be rolled to the

[2] C. W. Haskins, *The Argonauts of California* (New York, 1890), 14-15 and 47.

wharf and stowed for shipment, were still better.

One passenger spent much of his time making sheet-iron scoops, to which long poles were to be attached. Thus equipped, he would take his station under a shade tree on the river bank and there, safe from the sun and from the danger of wetting his feet, scoop up the golden sands.

The gold seekers put great faith in mechanical devices for extracting the gold from the sand and soil with which "unfortunately" it was mixed. They were of all varieties and patterns, made of copper, iron, brass, and zinc. Some were to be worked by a crank; others, more pretentious, by two cranks. One machine, which excited the envy of all beholders, was like a huge fanning mill, with sieves arranged to assort the gold ready for bottling. Chunks too large for the sieves would be consigned to the pork barrel.

This machine required the service of an assistant to turn the crank, while the owner busied himself shoveling in the pay dirt and pumping water. It belonged to a citizen of Cambridge, Massachusetts, who had prudently brought along his colored servant to assist him in operating it. Upon arrival at San Francisco, however, it was quietly abandoned on the beach, where along with a vast medley of other contrivances, it was soon washed out into deep water to furnish amusement for the shrimps and clams of the ocean bed.

Our own author supplies one pertinent footnote in this connection. Among the many "useless" items of property with which his party had outfitted itself at Boston was an immense augur, "with a very elaborate extension stem, with which we had intended to prospect the lower regions to any desired depth for the yellow metal." This, along with a quantity of sheet-iron gold washers, "made for the purpose of separating large quantities of gold from the shining sands," was abandoned somewhere along the Upper Platte, "Either of the above articles," Shaw dryly observes, "would have been about as useful in a gold mine as a bull in a china shop."

One of the commonest mistakes made by the emigrants was that of overburdening themselves with equipment and provisions, which wore down their oxen or horses, slowed their passage, and sooner or later ended in abandonment along the way. Enlightening in this connection are some of the observations of Captain Howard Stansbury, who led a government survey party from Fort Leavenworth to Great Salt Lake in the summer of 1849.[3] "We have been in company with emigrants the whole day," he wrote on June 12, when midway between Fort Leavenworth and Fort Kearney. "The road has been lined to a long extent with their wagons, whose white covers, glittering in the sunlight, resembled at a distance ships upon the ocean." Stansbury had encountered a French trader named Brulet, eastward bound from Fort Laramie to St. Louis with a pack train of buffalo robes. He reported that he had been forty days on the road and in that time had met not less than 4000 wagons westward bound, averaging four persons to the wagon. This same day (June 7) Stansbury also met a small party of emigrants who, having already "seen the elephant" were returning to St. Louis.[4] Of the road ahead, they reported that wagons could be bought for $10 to $15 apiece, and provisions for almost nothing at all. "So much," comments Stansbury, "for arduous enterprises rashly undertaken, and prosecuted without previous knowledge or suitable preparation."

[3] *Exploration and Survey of the Valley of the Great Salt Lake of Utah. . . .* (Senate exec. Doc. No. 3, Special sess., 1851); U.S. serial 608.
[4] *Ibid*, 18-19. "To see the elephant" meant to be discouraged, disillusioned, or, in modern phraseology, "fed up."

These conditions were reported almost at the outset of the Plains journey, and the farther the emigrants went the more common they became. At Fort Kearney, where Stansbury's party laid up for three days, a "spring carriage" left behind by an emigrant was obtained for Lieutenant Gunnison, who was ill. "Such abandonments are very common," observes Stansbury, "most of these sanguine and adventurous companies, by the time they get thus far, beginning to find out that they have started on their journey with more than they can contrive to carry. In order to lighten their load most of them dispose of everything they can possibly spare, and at almost any price. Flour and bacon, for example, had been sold as low as one cent per pound; and many, being unable to sell at that price, had used their meat for fuel."

A month later (July 19) on the second day westward from Fort Laramie, Stansbury reported this condition: "We passed today the nearly consumed fragments of about a dozen wagons that had been broken up and burned by their owners; and near them was piled up in one heap from 600 to 800 weight of bacon, thrown away for want of means to transport it farther. Boxes, bonnets, trunks, wagon wheels, whole wagon bodies, cooking utensils,

and, in fact, almost every article of house-
hold furniture, were found from place to
place along the prairie, abandoned for the
same reason."

Two days later still (July 21) "the road,
as usual, was strewn with fragments of broken and burnt wagons, trunks, and immense
quantities of white beans, which seemed to
have been thrown away by the sackful, their
owners tired of carrying them farther, or
afraid to consume them, from danger of the
cholera....stoves, gridirons, moulding-planes
and carpenters' tools of all sorts were to be
had at every stop for the mere trouble of
picking them up."

As yet, we have heard nothing of dead
horses and oxen. The goods and wagons
were abandoned, of course, to lighten the
burden of the animals, in the hope that they
would endure to the end of the journey. But
in the terrible trek down the Humboldt, or
across the desert from Winnemucca for those
who elected to go that way, the animals
perished of hunger or thirst in ever increasing numbers, so that the road was strewn
with their carcasses. As the beasts collapsed
the owners abandoned them to die of thirst
or to be torn to pieces by the wolves, only
rarely, apparently, troubling to end their
torture with a merciful bullet. When the

last wagons could no longer be pulled along, the emigrants either mounted such animals as remained or trudged along on foot, as necessity might dictate.

Some parties were better prepared than others, of course, to cope with the difficulties the journey entailed. Yet even those who possessed ample means and had thought to foresee and provide for every need were likely to come to grief through factors beyond their power to control. The "Boston Pack Company," as Shaw's party was commonly called, commanded ample funds, and an unusual degree of intelligence and thrift, yet it early came to grief, and in the end escaped disaster only by herculean effort.

In its case, most of the difficulties encountered, aside from those inevitable to the undertaking, proceeded from unwise planning and too blind reliance upon the advice of an incompetent leader. For one thing, the company was too large; for another, it was a joint stock company, all of whose property was held in common ownership, instead of each member owning and controlling his own property. All experience of overland travel emphasized the difficulty of conducting large parties; equally, all experience taught that individuals should remain together only as long as self interest dictated, with freedom of those concerned to secede or to form other combinations at will.

These things and the usual blunders of over-equipment and visionary planning apart, the Boston party's troubles seem chiefly to have been the infliction of their leader, Captain Joseph Thing. Despite our author's flattering account, his attainments and experience were considerably less than ideal. An ocean mariner and captain, he had joined the expedition of Nathaniel Wyeth, builder of Fort Hall in 1834. Wyeth was a typical Yankee, shrewd and enterprising and possessed of tremendous energy. If Thing had any other experience of the West than the Wyeth expedition afforded, we have been able to find no trace of it; and the greater such experience may have been, the less excusable his mistakes of leadership of the Boston Company became.

Presumably by his advice, it was decided to travel horseback, with a supply of pack-mules to carry the equipment and supplies, and with a drove of cattle to be killed en route for food. A principal motive for dispensing with wagons was the greater speed and mobility of horses and pack mules; but no one seems to have perceived that this advantage would be largely nullified by the necessity of accommodating the rate of travel to the pace of the accompanying herd of cattle.

Another sorry blunder, directly attributable to Captain Thing, was the preparation at Boston of a supply of wooden trunks to contain the multifarious articles of equipment and to be borne on the backs of the pack mules. If Captain Thing was in fact an experienced mountain man he must have known the consequences which this equipment would entail. The rigid trunk frames so galled the backs of the mules within the first few days of travel as to reduce them to a condition which shocked even the hardened sensibilities of veteran plainsmen who observed them.

Arrived at Independence, Captain Thing perpetrated the crowning folly of purchasing a drove of young mules. "In selecting horses, mules, or oxen for this expedition," Lansford Hastings had warned, "none should be taken which are under five or over ten years of age."[5] Although Thing may not have read this particular advice, as a veteran mountain man "who had crossed the plains many times," according to Shaw, he should have been at least as aware of its force as

[5] Lansford P. Hastings, The *Emigrant's Guide to Oregon and California*. . . . (Cincinnati, 1845) 145. Facsimile reproduction, Princeton, N. J., 1932.

Hastings, who was very far from being a veteran plainsman.

Both Shaw and Kimball Webster, who accompanied the Boston Pack Company, have left records of the sad condition of the pack mules. More revealing, perhaps, is the comment of an outsider, Captain Stansbury, on this subject. On June 12 he wrote: "We passed a Company from Boston consisting of 70 persons, 140 pack and riding mules, a number of riding horses, and a drove of cattle for beef. The expedition, as might be expected, and as is too generally the case, was badly conducted; the mules were overloaded and the manner of securing and arranging the packs elicited many a sarcastic criticism from our party, most of whom were old and experienced mountain men, with whom the making up of a pack and the loading of a mule amounted to a science."

A week later (June 19) at Fort Kearney he recorded: "The pack company from Boston, which had passed us on the route, and which we found encamped here on our arrival, left before our departure. As they had been entirely unaccustomed to the operation of packing, their mules, as was to be expected, were in a most horrible condition, with galled backs and sides that made one shudder to behold. The proper mode of arranging the load of their suffering animals is an art taught only by experience. These people, though belonging to a race famous for foresight and calculation, had, like others from less thrifty and managing portions of the Union, been selling and giving away all they could dispense with."

With the animals in such condition, at South Pass Thing led his trusting followers away from the regular highway into the midst of some of the most formidable mountains in North America. Here, hopelessly lost, they frittered away almost two weeks of precious time, enough to spell the difference between safe arrival in California and being trapped east of the Sierras with consequent starvation and death, as the Donner party had been trapped in 1846.

After twelve days of such wandering, the emigrants ignored their leader and found their way back to the highway without the benefit of guidance. Little cause for wonder that, as Kimball Webster records, they derisively named this portion of their route the "Thing Cut-Off."

In crossing the Plains proper timing was an essential element. If the journey were too prolonged, animals and provisions gave out, and this plight impended over the Boston Pack Company soon after its emergence from the mountain by-way it had followed. Accordingly the decision was reached to send a detachment in advance to purchase provisions in California and return with them to meet the main party. Our author was selected as one of the members of this party, a fact which affords incidental evidence of his standing among his associates. Since his narrative ends with the return meeting with the main party, it affords no information of the progress and vicissitudes of the latter beyond the point on Raft River in southern Idaho, where the advance detachment left it.

Reuben Cole Shaw, our author, lived the kind of career Americans are fond of idealizing. He was born at South Boston, March 14, 1826. His father died while the child was still too young to remember ever seeing him, leaving a widowed mother without means and with three small children to rear. As the result of this misfortune he became a "bound" boy, in keeping with the fashion of his time, and such he remained until he was nearly grown to manhood. Subsequently he became a carpenter's apprentice; eventually he achieved the rank of master carpenter and joiner, and this calling he followed for many years.

On May 2, 1847 he married Rebecca P. Smith and in due course of time five children were born to the couple. The first-born, Walter C. Shaw was a babe less than a year old when the young father determined to join in the gold rush to California in the hope of bettering his fortune. Shaw remained in California two years but like many others fortune eluded his eager search and he rejoined his family in Boston late in 1851 bringing little or no gold.

In its stead, he had acquired a wealth of experience, and he had made an observation which influenced his further career. On his western pilgrimage he had noted the surpassing advantages which residents of the Middle West enjoyed, and in March, 1853 he turned his back upon his native city to establish a new home in Ross County, Ohio. Three years later, for reasons no longer remembered or recorded, he migrated to Kossuth County in northwestern Iowa. This was then the extreme edge of frontier settlement, with Sioux massacres and warfare still in the lap of the future. After five years of unavailing struggle with this environment, he determined to return to Ross County. En route, late in the autumn he "landed, or rather stranded" in Farmland, in eastern Indiana, a dozen miles east of Muncie, practically penniless and with an ailing wife and a brood of five small children to support.

All unwitting, the desperate thirty-five year old pioneer had found his California. For him Farmland proved to be the end of the rainbow. The place where he had "foundered" became his permanent home, where he was to reside for more than forty years. Here he won financial security and before many years achieved the status of a leading citizen of his community. In the various capacities of farmer, poultry merchant, miller, financier, educator, counsellor, and neighbor, he made himself a leader not merely in business but in all the various activities which tended to uplift and improve the lives of those with whom his lot had been cast. When he died, on February 21, 1903, the local paper devoted half of its first page to the recital of his obituary, in addition to which his physician and admiring friend of forty-two years standing, Dr. L. N. Davis, indited a two-column personal tribute to his character and activities. The distinction he had won in life still follows him. Elderly residents of the community still speak of him in terms of highest praise; the attractive rural home he created still shelters the family of a great-grandson; and the prominent lot in beautiful Woodlawn Cemetery in which his remains were interred upholds the distinction of being the only burial plot in the entire cemetery which is permitted to be inclosed within an iron fence.

"It is better to be first in a little Iberian village," Caesar is reputed to have said, "than second even in Rome." Our author was no Caesar and his long life was lived devoid of fame in the larger sense. For almost four decades, however, he enjoyed the status of leadership and of assured affection and admiration in his own home community. He was unfailing in his support of all good causes, sparing neither effort nor purse in promoting them. Solider or more substantial success than he achieved can come to no American citizen.

Several years before his death Shaw's health became precarious and he withdrew from active business pursuits. On July 5, 1895, publication of his California narrative was begun in the Farmland *Enterprise*, continuing until the last installment on September 20. No editorial comment introduced the story, and none accompanied its conclusion. Whether editorial exigencies or the decision of the author terminated the narrative abruptly with the main party still engaged in crossing the Nevada desert, can now only be surmised.

WHERE THE BOOK WAS WRITTEN
The Home of Reuben Cole Shaw. Reproduced from a recent photograph

The qualities of the narrative itself require some comment. In certain respects its defects are outstanding enough; in certain others these are matched by offsetting excellencies. The historian of the Gold Rush who seeks to follow the day by day journey of the Boston Pack Party finds himself baffled almost at the outset. If Shaw possessed a diary of the journey, as one might readily infer from his frequent employment of definite dates, he was sadly careless about consulting it. Nor are his errors confined to the matter of dates, as the informed reader of his narrative can quickly determine. The obituary notices published at the time of Shaw's death in 1903 dwell on his excellent memory, his studious habits of mind, and his antiquarian tastes. The errors both of commission and of omission which characterize his narrative serve to convince the present editor that it was written from memory only, without benefit of reference to any contemporary diary.

The narrative makes no mention either of Fort Kearney or Fort Laramie, the two civilized stations the party encountered between Independence and California. Although the route from Independence to California was crowded with emigrants, encounters with whom were necessarily frequent, Shaw mistakenly remembers that after several hundred miles of travel, including a three-day lay-over at Fort Kearney, "no white men except those of our own party had been seen. It seemed that we were the sole occupants of that vast wilderness."

More curious still is the complete omission of any mention of the Granite State Company, 30 strong, from nearby New Hampshire, whose members traveled in company with Shaw's own Mount Washington Mining Company. Fortunately for our editorial task Kimball Webster, a member of the Granite State Company, kept a journal which has been published. More methodical and prosaic than Shaw's narrative, comparison with its daily entries permits the correction of Shaw's recital in the matter of dates and certain other details. The report of Captain Stansbury, whose scientific expedition was journeying as far as Great Salt Lake during the weeks the Boston Pack Party was proceeding westward, and the monumental compilation of Georgia Read and Ruth Gaines on the Gold Rush supply further incidental information.[6]

[6] *Gold Rush. The Journals, Drawings, and other Papers of J. Goldsborough Bruff, Captain, Washington City and California Mining Association, April 2, 1849-July 20, 1851* (2 vols., New York, 1944). Captain

Quite apart from accuracy of detailed narration is the quality which gives its chief value to Shaw's narrative. Unlike most matter-of-fact diarists, he wrote his impressions of the journey mellowed by the passage of almost half a century. An ardent admirer of Nature, his memory retained vivid pictures of impressive mountain scenery and of the picturesque life of the Indians encountered in the course of the journey. Viewed as an impressionistic picture of the scenes and experiences attendant upon the overland journey, his narrative is far more interesting and perhaps no less valuable than the more usual recital of routine facts recorded by those emigrants who kept a daily journal.

When the story had been published in the weekly issues of the Farmland *Enterprise*, various friends urged the author to revise it for publication in book form. Weakened in health and in eyesight, however, he lacked the inclination to undergo the work of revision and the narrative was issued by the *Enterprise* press in 1896, substantially as it had been printed in the newspaper. Comparison of sample pages of the book with the corresponding newspaper narrative discloses

Bruff, who was adept at drawing pictures, presents a picture of the Boston Pack Company as it toiled along the trail on a day in July, 1849.

that some slight changes were made from the text of the latter. Apparently these pertained chiefly to matters of punctuation, paragraphing, and other like details of the printer's art, and were dictated by the printer rather than by the author of the book.

The effort to determine how many copies of the book were printed and what became of them was rewarded with a certain measure of success. Mr. Lee Shaw, grandson of the author and a small boy at the time the book was printed, thinks his grandfather did not publish the book with any expectation of selling it. Instead he kept the copies in a large box in his home and gave them away freely to friends and employees, as well as to associates of the gold-rush journey. His memory of the size of the box which contained the books suggests the estimate that it may have contained 200 copies or more.

Mr. Guy McIntyre of Farmland, veteran local historian and antique and book dealer lends a certain degree of support to this estimate. He supposes that about 300 copies were printed and he definitely remembers what became of some of them. He relates that Shaw did offer copies of the book for sale but not meeting with success he commissioned McIntyre to sell them at the price of 50 cents, of which he was to retain one-half as his commission. Even at this price few copies could be sold, however, and finally Grant Spillers bought the remaining stock of books and, as McIntyre thinks, junked them.

This last detail may be incorrect, for the books today are in moderate demand and in moderate supply. An Indianapolis collector who formerly came from Winchester, the nearby county seat town, has recently advertised for copies of the book. Lee Shaw recalls that a few years ago some one came to the neighborhood and bought at a moderate price as many copies as he could persuade the local possessors to part with. Pertinent in this connection is the present editor's copy, which was given him a quarter century ago by William H. Murray, an energetic and veteran collector and dealer in Americana. Murray's method of operating was to establish himself temporarily in some central city or town and from it canvas the adjacent area for books, manuscripts, and other historical materials for resale to his library and other customers. It is a reasonable surmise that he thus acquired a number of copies of the Shaw narrative, one of which was presented to the writer of these lines.

The varying bits of evidence which have been accumulated point to the conclusion that while the original edition of the book is an obscure item, it is not really a rare one. Yet the still-existing file of the Farmland *Enterprise* in which the narrative was first presented is unique, and copies of the book are commonly unknown or inaccessible. No information of a second printing of the book has been found, and the data already cited concerning the absence of demand for the first edition seems to justify the presumption that no succeeding one exists.

Inclusion of the narrative in the Lakeside Classics series of western Americana, therefore, will give it a new and broader circulation than it has hitherto enjoyed. "To those who court adventure and love to view from lofty mountain heights the wonders of primeval things," wrote Mr. Shaw in 1896, "it [the narrative] may prove interesting; while to those who care less for the grandeur and beauty of nature it will probably be of little interest." If the writer had lived until 1949, he would probably have appraised his narrative more highly. By it he has supplied an interesting recital of gold-rush days and ways, which gave birth to the commonwealth of California, still proudly known as the Golden State.

The Editor in 1948, like the author almost ninety years earlier, found the quiet town of Farmland an exceedingly pleasant and friendly community. To Guy McIntyre, historian and antiquarian; to Mr. and Mrs. Carson E. Retter; to Lee Shaw, grandson of the author, and to Mrs. Fred Shaw, wife of great-grandson, Fred Shaw, the Editor's gratitude is expressed for their friendly reception and their efforts to aid him with information. Particularly indispensable was the aid rendered by Roy Webster, veteran editor of the *Enterprise*, in granting access to the file of that paper, which contains the first printing of the narrative, the obituary of Mr. Shaw, and other pertinent data. I wish also to acknowledge the assistance of Mr. Russell Martin of Detroit, who drew the map which depicts the route of the gold seekers.

ACROSS THE PLAINS

IN

FORTY-NINE.

~~~~~~

BY

R. C. SHAW.

~~~~~~

FARMLAND, IND.:
W. C. WEST, PUBLISHER.
1896.

Introductory

AT the earnest request of relatives and some of my most intimate friends I contributed to the Farmland Enterprise, in 1895, a series of articles under the caption of "Across the Plains in Forty-Nine."

As the effort was kindly received by the readers of that popular local journal, and favorably mentioned by those in whose judgment I had confidence, I was again solicited, and finally consented, to revise and publish the same in book form, in order that the reminiscences might the better be preserved by those for whom it was written.

After rounding up seventy years of a very busy life, however, I find myself with impaired eyesight and health, leaving me but little strength, and even less inclination, to express myself on paper; therefore this little volume makes no pretensions to literary merit.

I have endeavored to describe nature as I saw it, and in a commonplace way give a brief account of the perils and pleasures which I, and those who were associated with me, experienced during an overland journey from Boston to California in 1849.

To those who court adventure, and love to view from lofty mountain heights the wonders of primeval things, it may prove interesting; while to those who care less for the grandeur and beauty of nature it will probably be of little interest.

Across the Plains
in Forty-nine

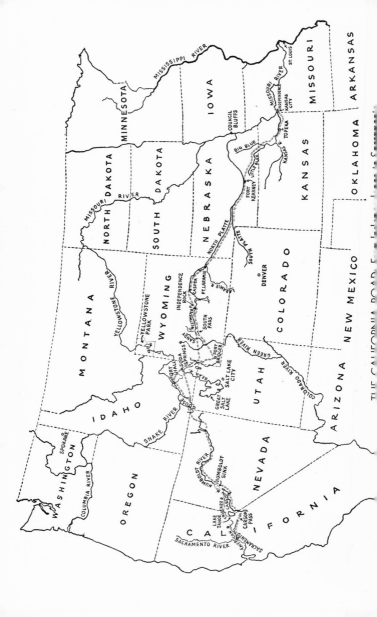

THE CALIFORNIA ROAD

Across the Plains
in Forty-nine

—

Chapter 1

Discovery of Gold in California—The Resulting Fever
and the Remedy—Formation of Companies for the
New Eldorado—The Grand Exodus by Land and
Sea—Dangers of an Overland Journey.

I HAVE often been solicited by my friends
to give a brief account of my travels and
adventures while crossing the plains to
California in 1849, through a country where
Indians held full sway, and who were known
to be very hostile and extremely jealous of
all white men who should dare venture within their boundaries; across a region of beautiful prairies, noble rivers, majestic mountains,
deep, dark and impassable canyons, dry and
barren deserts, vast fields of wild sage, snow-
capped peaks, ancient volcanic craters and
lava fields, hot and boiling springs, beautiful
parks, valleys and lakes, and where seem
gathered together the *mightiest monuments* of
the world's great wonders.

3

By referring back to 1849 we find all the vast region lying between the Missouri River and the Pacific Ocean uninhabited except by roving bands of Indians, whose habits and modes of life were as little known as was the character of the country which they occupied.

But few white men, at the time of which we write, had ever ventured beyond the fertile rolling prairies, forming the eastern portions of what are now the great States of Kansas and Nebraska.[1]

Fremont, by order of the United States Government in 1842, explored the country along the line of the Kansas and Nebraska[2] rivers as far as the South Pass, climbing the mountain peak which bears his name, and returned the same season.

Later explorations conducted by Fremont, in which he suffered untold hardships and the loss, by starvation, of all his animals and a large part of his men, resulted in nothing,

---

[1] This statement is accurate only in a relative sense. Prior to 1849 the country between the Missouri River and the Pacific Ocean had been extensively explored, and the reports of Fremont's expeditions in particular had obtained widespread popular reading. Many emigrants, too, had gone from the States to Oregon or to California, as well as Mormons to Utah. Compared with the subsequent flood of settlement however, the western country was relatively unknown and unsettled before 1849.

[2] The Platte, formerly often called the Nebraska River.

except as to the geography of the country traversed, and to confirm the opinion at that time entertained that the whole area lying west of the Missouri River was a barren waste, destitute of everything that contributes to the wants of civilized man.[3]

In 1845 a resolution was offered in the U. S. Senate by Hon. Thomas H. Benton, providing for an appropriation of $50,000 to enable Fremont to continue his explorations. The Senate refused to adopt the resolution, giving as a reason that it was a barren country and not worth the money. Here, then, was a country of vast extent—more than forty times as large as the State of Indiana—owned by and lying in sight of the most progressive nation on earth, yet our representatives in Congress, only fifty years ago, considered it as being almost worthless.[4]

[3] This summary of Fremont's explorations does considerably less than justice to his achievements. For more adequate accounts see the *Dictionary of American Biography*, and Allan Nevins, *Fremont; Pathmaker of the West* (New York, 1939).

[4] There is some further inaccuracy in these statements. The one concerning the appropriation presumably refers to Fremont's first expedition, in 1842. By his reports on this and on his second expedition of 1843-44 he captivated the imagination of the nation, and with war with Mexico impending Senator Benton encountered no difficulty in obtaining the appropriation for the third expedition, begun in the summer of 1845.

In 1847 the Mormons commenced their migrations to Salt Lake, in what is now the State of Utah, which, in view of the barren and forbidding aspect of the country, they named Deseret.[5] Here they supposed themselves to be out of the territory of the United States, beyond the reach of interference by any other government, and left to pursue their peculiar religious rites in their own way.

At the close of the Mexican War, in 1848, Utah, together with New Mexico, Nevada and California, were ceded by Mexico to the United States, and, subsequently, Arizona was acquired by purchase.[6]

These new acquisitions, containing over one million square miles, when added to former possessions formed a vast mountain region about fifteen hundred miles square, which was traversed by two high mountain ranges running north and south through its entire length. Between the mountain barriers lies the Great Basin, or Salt Lake Val-

[5] The word Deseret was derived from the *Book of Mormon* and meant "the honey-bee."

[6] The Mexican cession of 1848 embraced the present day states of California, Nevada, Utah, and much the greater portions of Arizona and New Mexico, about 550,000 square miles. Subsequently, in December, 1853, by the Gadsden Purchase, the United States acquired an additional area (about 45,500 square miles) in southern New Mexico and Arizona, comprising the territory south of the Gila River.

ley, into which rivers and streams of considerable size flow from the mountains, where they sink or are lost in the desert sands, as no outlet for them has ever been discovered.

This Great Basin was described by Fremont as being six hundred miles wide, eight hundred miles long, and elevated above the sea about five thousand feet. It is surrounded by lofty mountains and, though the interior was almost unknown, was believed to contain rivers and lakes which had no communication with the sea. It was also supposed to contain unexplored deserts and oases, and savage tribes which had never been seen or described by civilized man.

Later explorations proved it to be almost destitute of vegetable or animal life. It being of volcanic origin, there were found long stretches of ashes of an unknown depth, and also extensive lava fields, where vegetation failed to find an abiding place.

Prior to the time of which we write, adventurous hunters and trappers had plied their vocation along the line of the Missouri River to its source in the mountains, there striking the head waters of the Columbia and following that stream to the trading posts of the American Fur Company on the Pacific Coast, where they squandered the proceeds from the sale of their peltries in riotous living, returning the next season over the same route to St. Louis, where they spent the winter as hale fellows well met. They traveled in parties of three or more, in order to better protect themselves from hostile Indians. Their rifles furnished them with food and they slept under the stars without shelter, enjoying perfect health in the pure mountain air, and were never so happy as when fraternizing with, or fighting, Indians.

Their trapping expeditions were both profitable and enjoyable, and, with proper economy they should have become wealthy, but an ingenious somebody (whose name is lost to history) about the year 1846, discovered that silk could be used for covering hats, and the occupation of the trapper was gone forever; but, being bold hunters, skilled in woodcraft and conversant with the habits of Indians, besides having some knowledge of the dialect of the different tribes, their services were in demand as guides and hunters by parties while crossing the plains in 1849, and they were eager to avail themselves of any opportunity of going to California on a free pass.[7]

[7] This paragraph supplies a none too adequate account of the group of trappers and traders commonly known as the "Mountain Men." For fuller accounts of the subject see *Dictionary of American History*; Dale Morgan, *Great Salt Lake* (Indianapolis, 1947), Chap. 6. The use of silk instead of beaver skins in the manufacture of hats began a dozen years earlier than 1846.

Gold was discovered on the American River in California by Thomas W. Marshall on the 19th of January, 1848.

The news of that important event reached the Atlantic Coast by the way of Cape Horn in September following, but the glowing accounts were not verified until January, 1849 —one year from the date of the discovery of the precious metal.[8]

By this time nuggets and specimens of gold were on exhibition in show windows; fabulous accounts were given of fortunes made in a day—of renegade Mexicans riding half-wild horses to the mountains, picking out chunks of gold with their bowie-knives and returning to Mexico laden with wealth.

The Digger Indians, the lowest of created beings, were represented as having thrown away their arrows and filling their quivers with gold dust.

Sailors on the Pacific Coast deserted their vessels for the new Eldorado. Ships were fitted out from Atlantic ports in the least possible time for a voyage of fifteen thousand

[8] The discovery of gold in California was made by James W. Marshall on January 24, 1848. Public excitement over the discovery was set off by President Polk's annual message to Congress December 5, 1848. On the subject of how the news of the discovery was carried to the East, see *Kit Carson's Autobiography* (The Lakeside Classics, Chicago, 1935), 123.

miles around Cape Horn to California, and
they were crowded with passengers.

The California fever of '49 was raging in
all its fury, and the only remedy seemed to
be a change of climate with the least possible delay.

As the reports of the wonderful discovery
of gold were fully confirmed, everybody
became excited. Merchants closed out
their business, clerks left their employers,
mechanics packed their tools, lawyers gave
up their practice, preachers bade adieu to
their flocks and all joined the grand pro-
cession.

Over twenty thousand persons left Boston
for California in '49—a large majority of
them by water. While the voyage around
Cape Horn by water could be made with
comparative safety, a journey across the
plains was thought to be extremely hazardous; yet, in view of prospective wealth,
coupled with a love of adventure and a desire to see and explore the mysteries of the
unknown West, there were many who were
willing to take the risk.

Up to the first day of November, 1849,
about five hundred vessels, each containing
more or less passengers besides their crews,
had arrived at San Francisco within the preceding year, and there were at that time

upwards of two hundred vessels on their way from Atlantic ports.

The Mount Washington Mining Company, of which the writer was a member, was organized and incorporated under the laws of Massachusetts, March 10th, 1849, and consisted of fifty members, the greater part of whom were residents of Boston and vicinity, though New Hampshire and Vermont were represented, each by two stalwart members.[9]

Dr. J. N. Haynes, a wealthy physician of twenty years' practice, joined us and volunteered his services as surgeon to our party. His motive in crossing the plains was to gratify his love of adventure and intense desire to travel in wild and unknown regions, where

[9] The names of 41 members of the Company are given in C. W. Haskins, *The Argonauts of California*, 411-12. Throughout his narrative Shaw makes no mention of the Granite State and California Mining and Trading Company, whose 29 members were chiefly New Hampshire men, many of them from Pelham, and which traveled in company with Shaw's own Mount Washington Company most of the way to California. One of its members, Kimball Webster, kept a journal which was published at Manchester, N.H. in 1917, entitled *The Gold Seekers of '49: A Personal Narrative of the Overland Trail and Adventures in California and Oregon from 1849 to 1854.* It supplements and corrects Shaw's narrative in many ways, and will be cited frequently in subsequent footnotes.

he could observe nature in all her majesty and wildness, while yet unshorn of its beauty by the hand of man, and, as he humorously expressed it, to enjoy a season of rest from his labors.

Applicants for membership in our company were subjected to rigid examination by the surgeon and many rejected on account of physical disability; yet it is a noteworthy fact that those who seemed the most robust and, to all appearances, best able to battle with the hardships of the journey, were the first to succumb to disease and death.

Joseph Thing, an old-time hunter and trapper of the mountains, who, in his wanderings, had crossed the plains many times along the usual route of the trappers, was engaged as guide for our company. His amiable disposition, his experience in mountain life, and his knowledge of Indian character and of the dialect of many of the tribes made him a valuable acquisition to our numbers.[10]

By the advice of our guide we determined to cross the plains with saddle-horses and pack-mules, for by this method we could

[10] On the career of Captain Joseph Thing and his "value" to the Company see *ante*, our Historical Introduction. Webster states that he received five dollars per member for piloting the Granite State Company to California. *Gold Seekers of '49*, 21.

more readily ford rivers, select camping places in isolated grassy spots, navigate among rocks and through canyons, climb and wind around steep mountain sides and through timber where it would be quite impossible for wagoners to make their way, while with a less elaborate outfit we expected to make better time than by any other mode of travel.

Before leaving Boston we secured for our journey such supplies as we supposed could not be readily obtained on the frontier.

Our company was composed of men from many different walks in life, among them lawyers, doctors, preachers, teachers, students, merchants, clerks, and mechanics. The larger number of them were in the prime of their manhood, though several students from institutions of learning were but little past their majority.

The mystery attached to the country which we were to traverse, the novelty of the undertaking, the prospect of lively adventure and, in some cases, the benefits that were expected to be derived from a change from the counting-room to life in the open air seemed to be the primary incentives to their crossing the plains.

While we formed the only company which left Boston by the overland route, many other organized companies purchased and fitted out ships and took their chances of an ocean voyage of about fifteen thousand miles around Cape Horn.

The *Edward Everett*, a fine ship, left Boston about ten days before the date of our departure, with a company of three hundred men, besides her crew of twenty officers and sailors. I had seriously thought of joining the party, for among its members were a number of my acquaintances; but, learning that a company was being organized to cross the plains, I abandoned all thoughts of a long ocean voyage, which promised nothing but threadbare adventure, with but little of mystery or novelty.

I may here digress and briefly give the reader something about the perils and pleasures experienced by the passengers of a noble ship.

The *Edward Everett* was nearly new and one of the finest ships of her time, while she was furnished with all the improved appliances of the age, and her owners were complimented on their choice of so fine a vessel.

After leaving Boston nothing worthy of mention occurred, except rough weather and much sea sickness among those who were unaccustomed to ocean voyages, until they reached the southern coast of Patagonia, in midwinter, and attempted to pass through the Straits of Magellan, which was always considered a dangerous undertaking for sailing ships, even in summer.

Here they were beset by adverse winds and currents, and finally abandoned all hope of forcing their ship through the straits, making the best of their way around Cape Horn in about sixty degrees of south latitude, encountering terrible gales, extreme cold, dense fogs, snow and ice.

On reaching the calmer waters of the Pacific it was discovered that many of the passengers were in the incipient stages of scurvy, which necessitated their entering the port of Valparaiso for supplies of fruit and vegetables.

The ship finally arrived at San Francisco, after a voyage lasting five and a half months, with a very debilitated lot of passengers.

I have many times congratulated myself because of the fact that I was not one of the passengers of the good ship *Edward Everett*.

Chapter 2

Off for California by Rail, River and Pack-Mule—
Seventeen Days from Boston to Independence—
Camping Among the Oaks—Seven of Our Party Die
of Cholera—A Long Delay—Breaking Mules—A
Ten-Dollar Ambulance—On the Trail—Horses Sto-
len by Thieves—A Discouraging Outlook—Mode of
Travel.

AFTER many vexatious delays, we left
Boston on the 17th of April by Boston and Albany railway, thence by
New York Central, arriving in Buffalo forty
hours from Boston. After waiting three days,
during which time we visited Niagara Falls,
we boarded a lake steamer for Sandusky;
thence by rail to Cincinnati, and next by
river steamer down the Ohio and up the Mississippi to St. Louis, where we changed boats
for Council Bluffs on the Missouri; but,
learning that the animals required for our
journey could not be obtained at that place,
we decided to make Independence, Mo., our
starting point, arriving there on the third
day of May.[11]

[11] Webster's account of the journey from Boston to
Independence is considerably more detailed than
Shaw's. Both accounts agree upon the dates of depar-
ture and of arrival at Independence; but Webster de-

Across the Plains in Forty=nine

After selecting the shortest and most direct route and improving all available opportunities for speed, we were seventeen days in making the distance from Boston to Independence, bringing in striking contrast the facilities for travel at the present time which the traveler can not fail to appreciate, for now, in the most luxurious cars on the best equipped railroads in the world, the anxious traveler is hurried along at the rate of fifty miles an hour, and reaches Independence from Boston in twice as many hours as we were days in covering the same distance. But at that time—only forty-seven years ago—there were no railroads or telegraphic lines reaching the Mississippi, and mails hadn't yet crossed the Missouri.

The third day from St. Louis we landed on the bank of the Missouri and buried two of the boat's crew, who had died of cholera, and on the night before reaching Independence, Nathan Watkins, one of our party, died of the same disease and was buried near the landing.

scribes the route followed from Buffalo as by steamboat to Detroit, thence by Michigan Central train to New Buffalo, thence by steamboat to Chicago, thence by canal packet to La Salle, and by river steamers from the latter place to St. Louis and Independence. It seems evident that Shaw's account of the journey from Boston to Independence is considerably erroneous.

We formed our camp in a fine grove of young oaks about two miles south of the river, and here we were destined to remain for more than forty days,[12] during which time we had thirteen cases of cholera and four deaths.

It is remarkable that, notwithstanding the depressing circumstances under which we were laboring and the gloomy prospects of the future, not one of our party was disposed to abandon the enterprise and return home.

While some of our men were caring for the sick, others were scouring the country for mules and horses to complete our outfit, for we were anxious to vacate the camp where cholera seemed to spring from the ground.[13]

We found the buying of such animals as was required in that sparsely settled country a difficult task, as the supply near at hand had been exhausted by parties making an earlier start, and they were only to be found after canvassing a large area of territory, which necessitated long rides.

[12] Actually, 38 days.

[13] Webster relates that Captain Thing and Lafayette Allen (the latter of the Granite State Company) had been sent on two weeks earlier to procure mules and cattle for the expedition, and that the mules were being herded by Mr. Sloan until the arrival of the emigrants. *Gold Seekers of '49*, 21 and 34.

Many of the mules purchased had seen service in the Mexican War, and, though poor in flesh, having been wintered without care or shelter, they proved to be the most serviceable animals in our train.

There were also mules in our outfit which had never been handled, and in breaking them to saddle and pack many valiant riders found themselves in very undignified positions.[14] A number of our mules were never thoroughly subdued until reaching the alkali region, by which time they had worn themselves out and became food for coyotes.

While the sick were convalescing, our camp presented a bustling scene, all being occupied in completing the arrangements for our journey in the wilderness. As it was evident that at least two of our men would be unable to take to the saddle for several days, and they being very desirous of changing locations, the doctor suggested an ambulance. We therefore purchased the running-gear of an old spring wagon, which had seen many years of hard service and been thrown aside as worthless, though the owner made it

[14] "They were young mules which had neven been halter-broken, and were about as wild as the deer on the prairie. A wild, unbroken mule is the most desperate animal that I have ever seen." Webster, *Gold-Seekers of '49*.

19

appear very cheap at ten dollars. With a little rough lumber picked up at the Landing, hickory bows worked out with a dull ax, heavy muslin for a covering, a liberal supply of hay cut with a sheath-knife, and an old horse and harness that a Gypsy might envy, we had a vehicle in which the sick could ride with comfort and of which the boys were quite proud.

This forced delay might have proved fatal to our undertaking. We were warned by old frontiersmen of the danger of making so late a start, being told that the small streams would be dried up by the middle of summer, and that we might expect to find water only after long marches, in camping places where grass and fuel had been consumed by the immense number of travelers in advance of us.

It was represented to us that on the approach of the rainy season in California, which set in about the first of September, vast quantities of snow would fall in the mountains and that it would be quite impossible for us to get through them. We were also reminded of the fate of Fremont and his party when caught in the snows of the Sierra-Nevada mountains in 1846. While these warnings may have increased our anxiety to some extent, yet there was no thought of abandoning our cherished enterprise.

After an early breakfast on the 10th of
June, having had no new cases of cholera for
several days, we packed up for a start into the
wilderness, and yet it was high noon before
we succeeded in forcing some of the fractious
mules to take their packs out of the camp
where we had been so long delayed.[15]

The first night out we camped in detach-
ments along the bank of a small creek, the
foremost mess having made about fifteen
miles, while those in the rear were not more
than five or six miles out, and in this way we
traveled for several days, by which time our
mules became somewhat sobered, and we
then traveled and camped in a body. Our
mules, after being packed, were turned loose
and driven along by the guards.

The eighth day out we crossed the Kansas
River[16] at a ford about one hundred miles

[15] According to Webster the start was made on May
26. This discrepancy may perhaps be explained by the
fact that the party, as Shaw relates, moved in detach-
ments, considerably spread out. "It took as many men
to pack a mule as could stand around it, and we were
obliged to choke many of them before we could get the
saddle upon their backs. . . . Several of our company
were quite badly disabled by working with them, so that
they were unable to assist in packing." *Gold Seekers of
'49*, 36-37.

[16] Crossing the Kaw, or Kansas River was an important event in the annals of all California-bound travelers.
The fording place was near present-day Rossville,

21

from Independence and camped for the night on the north bank, where five of our best horses were reported missing the next morning. The most of the day was spent in pursuit of the animals, but they were never found, though we obtained the best of evidence that they were stolen by white men.

Having lost five horses and being about to enter the country of the Pawnee Indians, we began to see the necessity of a more thorough organization, and at a meeting of the company our guide was elected commander-in-chief, all agreeing to abide by such rules as he saw fit to adopt, and we soon found ourselves in complete working order. Our guide was at once dubbed "General," and he retained the title to the day of his death, which occurred several years later. Guards were arranged for both night and day. Each man was assigned his duties and was expected to execute them with promptness. Powder and lead were distributed to all; instructions given as to the care of our firearms, with orders to keep them loaded and ready for any emergency; and we were also exercised at target practice.

about a dozen miles west of Topeka. Webster's journal gives June 4 and 5 as the date of crossing of the Boston party.

On June 22d we were crossing a beautiful prairie, between the Kansas and Platte rivers, and were making excellent time; but just as we had selected our camp for the night one of the rear guards came in and reported two of our men, Professor Nye and D. W. Hinckley, stricken with cholera five miles behind and lay dying by the wayside.

This intelligence struck our camp like a thunderbolt, for we were congratulating ourselves on being done with cholera; but here was the prospect of losing two more of our esteemed members and of another long delay. Owing to this disease we were already forty or fifty days behind, and, as the game had been driven from the road by earlier hunters, our supplies were being rapidly consumed, and we were liable to be caught in the early snows on the mountains, making the outlook, to say the least, very discouraging.

Five of our comrades had previously become the prey of this dread disease, and yet, like a sleuth-hound, it was still pursuing us. But there was no time to indulge in regrets.

The doctor and four men started back at once to the aid and support of our sick brothers, taking along the packs which belonged to them, as their pack-mules had been driven into the main camp. The other members of the mess to which the sick men belonged had remained with them.

Medical treatment, sympathy and brotherly care proved of no avail. Both patients passed into a state of collapse before midnight and died early next morning.

Their bodies were laid out in clean clothes, after which they were sewed up in their blankets, and at high twelve buried in one grave, over which (utilizing the rocks in the vicinity) we erected a neat and substantial cairn.

The main camp having been notified early in the morning of passing events, and, acting on the advice of the doctor, who wished to keep the men from brooding over the past, it was arranged for the company to travel this day the same as usual, and for those in the rear, after burying the dead, to join the main body at night.

After performing the last sad rites over the grave of our lamented comrades and burning all the clothing in which they had died, we packed up and were on the road by 2 o'clock p. m., intending to reach the main camp without a halt.

Being one of the party, I was requested to ride the bell-horse for the pack-mules to follow, to which I readily assented; and it is possible that my anxiety to change locations from where the very air seemed thick with despondency, and the lonely position in which I was placed (being far in the lead), had something to do with the excellent speed made, as we arrived in camp, thirty miles away, before dark, demonstrating the fact that a mule could make six or seven miles an hour under a two-hundred-pound pack.

The sudden death of these two members of our party cast a gloom over our camp, and their taking off was deeply lamented. Professor Nye was about forty-five years of age and a gentleman in the truest sense. He had been teaching for more than twenty consecutive years. He was a very enthusiastic botanist and anticipated much enjoyment from a journey across the plains. D. W. Hinckley was probably twenty-one or twenty-two years of age, and a nephew of Professor Nye. He had just rounded up four years of college life, and undertook this journey at the solicitation of his uncle, who agreed to pay all the expenses of his trip. That both should be stricken with cholera at the same time and die within a few minutes of each other was beyond our comprehension.

Our company was divided into seven messes of six men each. The messes were known by numbers, and the members of each mess were assigned their duties, both while in camp and on the road. Each man was provided with a horse or mule to ride, and also a mule to carry his pack, which contained his wearing apparel, provisions, etc. We also had extra pack-mules—one in the care of each mess. One of them was packed with pork, another with rice, another with beans, another with ammunition, another with the medicine chest, and two with navy bread. These mules had pet names. They were known as "Pigtail," "Chinaman," "Beanpod," "Powder-Horn," "Pill-Bags" and "Cracker-Boxes."

Our mode of travel was as follows: We were aroused at early daybreak, the animals turned loose to graze, and breakfast was prepared and eaten with appetites that epicures might envy. At six o'clock the General and members of one mess, forming the advance guard, left camp and were generally one or two miles in advance of the main body. They were always on the lookout for Indians and game, and it was their duty to select the places for the noon halts and also for camping at night. The mules being packed and ready for the road, another mess of six men (one of them riding the bell-horse) moved out, and the pack-mules were driven after them. Two other messes took their stations —one on each flank to keep the mules in line—while the three remaining messes brought up the rear in three sections. If a mule threw his pack or got it misplaced, the first rear section took him in hand, adjusted his load and rushed him into the drove—the second section taking the place of the first, which fell in the rear.

It will be seen that by this method the members of each mess were always together and working in company, and that in the course of seven days they filled all the stations from the advance to rear guard in turn. The doctor, who was an excellent hunter, by common consent always formed one of the advance guard, which gave him a better opportunity to study geology and botany. He was often accused of breaking ranks and exploring the hills in order, as he said, "to find specimens to balance the pack on his mule."

In order to guard against accidents when on steep grades, our riding and pack-saddles were furnished with strong breast-straps, cruppers and very wide leather girths. Our animals were also provided with ropes about twenty-five feet long, with iron pickets attached, with which to tether them in any desired location.

Packs were held in place on the mules by strong surcingles, and, in addition to them, we used lash-ropes twenty feet long; yet,

27

with all the precaution we were able to take, it was three or four weeks after leaving the frontier before our wild mules acknowledged themselves conquered and ceased dumping their packs along the road.

Our riding saddles were of the kind called at that time the naked Spanish tree. They were without pads of any kind, but very light and strong. A sweat-cloth and blanket, folded to the proper size and placed on the back of the horse, formed the pad, and a blanket above the saddle, secured by a strong surcingle, formed the seat.

A becket, attached to the horn of the saddle for carrying a gun, and small waterproof holsters for revolvers and ammunition, completed the outfit.

Our saddle pads were the only blankets we had to protect us from the chilly mountain air during the night, and though at times they were sadly in need of being laundered, I think we slept none the less on that account.

Chapter 3

ON June 24th, signs of buffalo having
been seen for a day or two, the advance guard, which was composed of
the hunters of the company, started out before sunrise with the view of finding the game
while grazing in the valleys, it being the habit of these animals to retreat to the hills and
spend the heat of the day. Light guns were
exchanged for those better adapted to taking
large game, and there was also some temporary swapping of horses before the squad
set out with high hopes of success.

While traveling up a narrow belt of timber which skirted a small stream, we were
surprised at having a number of deer break
through our train on their way to the prairie.
The excitement and shooting which followed
their appearance resulted only in crippling
one of our mules so seriously that the animal
had to be shot and left to the coyotes.

Near nightfall, after a march of about twenty-five miles, we overtook the enthusiastic hunters, and there were eight weary, half-starved men, they not having had a particle of food since early morning. Nor had they seen a buffalo, or even a jack-rabbit.

On June 25th, we had a succession of rolling prairies and deep, miry streams, one of which was quite difficult to cross. Two of our wild pack-mules mired, stuck fast, and gave up to die; but, with a rope about the neck, they were pulled out more dead than alive, and the ordeal seemed to have changed their dispositions, as after their mud bath they became very tame and gentle.

During the noon halt we were visited by three Sioux hunters—the first Indians seen on our march. They had been on a hunting expedition along the Loup River, and, having met with very indifferent success, were returning to their camp with a very small quantity of dried venison, which they carried on their riding ponies. They eagerly accepted an invitation to take dinner with us, and became very friendly, seeming pleased to learn that the General was able to converse with them in their own tongue. They were fairly good-looking Indians, though their clothing was extremely abbreviated.

It was ascertained that the chief Indian (or the one who seemed to be the leader of the party) had, at some previous time, visited Council Bluffs, and the General suggested that possibly, for a consideration, they might be induced to take letters for us to some trading-post on the Missouri, and there left to take chances of reaching their destination by whatever conveyance might be found. The proposition was favorably received by most of the company, the Indians promising to deliver the letters to some trader at Council Bluffs, or at a place then called Chouteau's Landing.[17]

The General entertained but little doubt as to the favorable outcome of the project, and many of our party availed themselves of the opportunity of writing to their friends in the East, while others had no faith in the venture,

[17] Chouteau's Warehouse, or Landing was established in 1826 by Pierre Chouteau Jr. of the American Fur Company on the site of present-day Kansas City, Missouri. In 1838 a town-site was platted and the name Kansas City was given to the place.

A U.S. Army post was located briefly on the site of Council Bluffs in 1837. In 1847 the Mormons, migrating westward to Great Salt Lake, made the place a rendezvous and the modern city may be said to date from this time. Until 1853 it bore the name of Kanesville. Lewis and Clark in 1804 had held a council with Indians in this vicinity and from this circumstance the name Council Bluffs was given to the city by special act of the State Legislature in 1853.

but in time learned that an excellent chance
had been frittered away.

It was suggested that the letters, when completed, should be made up in a package, and
that the General negotiate with the Indians
for carrying them; but the Chief, having an
eye to the "main chance," objected to such an
arrangement. He looked upon the matter as
a retail business, and proposed to strike the
best possible bargain with each letter-writer
separately. He seemed to know nothing about
a wholesale, spot-cash deal, with a per cent.
off, but was determined to make the most of
the opportunity.

While he did not seem to be anxious for
money, there was nothing else in our outfit
but what he was willing to take, and at the
final settlement quite a quantity of second-
hand clothing, notions, tobacco and jewelry
changed hands, and the Indians generally got
whatever they fancied. Nothing less than a
calico shirt, of the pattern like I was then
wearing, appeared to them to be of the proper
value for carrying my letter. The Indians
got the shirt, and several months later I had
the satisfaction of knowing that my wife received the letter.

Our leading Indian, when dressed in a blue
calico shirt, with a wide navy collar; a pair of
antiquated pants, which were about ten inches

too short for his long legs; new and bright-colored suspenders, which he insisted on crossing in front; a red ribbon for a necktie, with bare head and naked feet, looked the prince of dudes. The other two Indians were not so elaborately dressed, but, comparing their outfit with the raiment in which they were introduced to us, they made a very good appearance.

The letters were finally made up in a package and directed to Boston, with a note attached requesting any one into whose hands it might fall to forward it eastward at the first convenient opportunity, and it was the middle of the afternoon when the three proud Sioux Indians set out on the first mail route ever established in what is now the great State of Nebraska.

The fact that the letters reached their destination proved that the trio of hunters (though full-blood Sioux Indians) were faithful to their trust, while in what way or by whom our letters, after leaving the hands of the Indians, were forwarded to the St. Louis postoffice will probably never be known.

After a hard day's work, we camped on the bluffs of a shallow stream bordered with timber, where, posted on a large tree, was found the following:

"NOTICE.—We camped here on the 10th day of May. Jim Lider went up the creek to

hunt deer and never came back. We found his dead body two miles up the creek after two days' hunt, his scalp, clothes and gun all gone. The Pawnees did it. Look out for the red devils.   JOHN SLADE,
                    Captain Otter Creek Co."

June 26th was extremely hot and sultry, and the march was very tedious and fatiguing. While preparing the camp for the night on the steep bluff of a timberless creek, we noticed a heavy bank of clouds in the west and could hear the ominous roll of distant thunder, indicative of a terrible storm.

Supper was hastily eaten and everything made snug for the night. The animals were secured to their pickets, the guards assigned their beats, and by this time the storm had found us.

We were treated to a grand display of electricity and the heaviest of thunder, while the rain seemed to vie with the wind in trying to see which could do the most damage and make us the most uncomfortable.

Tents offered but little protection from the storm, for, in spite of us, they were blown down and, together with the blankets, clothing, and cooking utensils, strewn about the prairie and many articles never found.

The ambulance, in which two of the men had taken refuge, was hurled down the steep

34

bluff, tumbling the occupants out as it descended, and landed in the river a total wreck.

It is almost unnecessary to state that we passed a sleepless night, shivering with cold, and were glad to see daylight.

It was 2 o'clock p. m. the next day before everything was gotten in shape to resume the journey. The weather being cool and delightful after the storm, the march was very interesting, as en route there was a succession of broad prairies, immense boulders, deep streams and sandy plains, which were completely honey-combed by prairie-dogs.

After thirty miles travel the Platte was sighted,[18] and two miles down the bluffs and across a fine bottom brought us to the river, where a feast awaited our arrival, the hunters having killed a fine buffalo cow and yearling calf, which they had neatly dressed and cut up ready for cooking; also had gathered chips

---

[18] On June 17, eight miles below Fort Kearney, according to Webster, who also places the fording of the South Platte on Thursday, June, 28. *Gold Seekers of '49*, 48 and 53. These dates are approximately confirmed by Howard Stansbury, whose party reached Fort Kearney on June 19 and found the Boston men already there. Stansbury remained at the fort three days, and the Boston party left it during this interval. *Exploration and Survey of the Great Salt Lake. . . .* Senate Exec. Doc. 3, Special Sess., 1851, p. 30.

for fuel, and in a very short time the air was laden with an appetizing odor.

It is somewhat remarkable that in traveling the distance from the Missouri River to the Sacramento no dense forests were discovered. With the exception of isolated cottonwood trees and small brush along the watercourses, but little timber was seen east of the Sweetwater, while at the base and on the lower slopes of the Wind River and Sierra Nevada mountains were scattering oaks and pines of low, spreading growth, with a stunted mass of brush near the timber line, while along the margin of the mountain streams were several varieties of willow, with the larger of which the beaver built his dam, while using the bark of the smaller varieties for his winter food.

On reaching the Platte, the General informed us that for three hundred miles along the river we should not find a particle of timber, and that the cooking would have to be done over a fire made from buffalo chips (the dried excrement of the buffalo), which, when used in the trapper's fireplace, proved a very satisfactory fuel.

For the benefit of the reader, I will briefly explain the manner in which the fireplace, or oven, of the trapper was constructed, when using buffalo chips as fuel along the Platte.

Selecting a spot a short distance from the steep river bank, a hole about six inches in diameter and eight to twelve inches deep was excavated. An air tunnel was then formed by forcing a ramrod horizontally from the river bank to the bottom of the cavity, giving the oven the required draught. In making a fire (after gathering a quantity of dry chips, which were found in abundance), a wisp of dry grass was lighted and placed at the bottom of the oven, opposite the air tunnel, feeding the flame with finely pulverized dry chips, which readily ignited. Then after filling the fireplace with broken chips and placing around the oven two or three small rocks on which to rest the cooking utensils, we had a combination which at first gave us a grand surprise, as but little smoke and only slight odor emitted from the fire, and we found, after having eaten our first meal cooked in this manner, that the prejudice previously entertained against buffalo chips as a fuel had vanished into thin air.

The Platte River at this point was over a half-mile wide, but had only about two feet of water at the deepest places. Quicksand formed the bed of the stream, into which our animals sank rapidly, but they soon learned to keep in motion while drinking from it.

Across the Plains in Forty-nine

The river valley, extending from one to three miles on either side, was composed of a rich, sandy loam, on which was growing the most luxuriant grasses and a great variety of flowering plants. The river bottoms were bordered by high and broken sand-bluffs, which presented a very barren appearance, and there was no timber in sight of our camp—not even a willow.

We were between three and four hundred miles on our journey, but no white men, except those of our own party, had been seen. It seemed that we were the sole occupants of that vast wilderness.[19]

We passed many villages of prairie-dogs, and found the little animals quite interesting,

[19] This paragraph contains a rather surprising error. The journals of Captain Stansbury and others disclose that hundreds of wagons were passing westward, not to mention parties of traders and of despairing emigrants who were returning eastward, or the stop which Shaw's party had made at Fort Kearney on June 17-19. Stansbury's party had encountered the Boston gold seekers on June 12, and again at Fort Kearney on June 19. On June 7, he records meeting a trader, Brulet, coming from Fort Laramie with a large quantity of buffalo robes for the St. Louis market. He had been 40 days on the road from Fort Laramie and estimated that he had met 4000 emigrant wagons toiling westward. Obviously Shaw's party had frequently encountered white men, both traders and emigrants, in their journey from Independence to this point.

but very shy. The Doctor, with all his skill as a marksman, failed to capture a specimen.[20]

We crossed the south fork of the Platte by fording. The treacherous quicksand kept the mules in constant motion, and they needed no urging when once started across.[21]

About the middle of the river we found an abandoned wagon sticking fast in the quicksand. The covering had been removed from the bows and the wheels were almost wholly submerged, while the bed was quietly resting on the bottom in nearly a foot of water.

[20] "We passed today through a large village or settlement of the prairie dog, extending in length not less than half a mile. These little animals are very shy, and at the first approach of a stranger hie themselves with all speed to their holes. . . . They are very hard to get, as they are never found far from their holes; and when shot, fall immediately into them, where they are generally guarded by a rattlesnake the usual sharer of their subterranean retreat. Several were shot by us in this situation, but when the hand was about to be thrust into the hole to draw them out, the ominous rattle of this dreaded reptile would be instantly heard, warning the intruder of the danger he was about to incur." Stansbury, *Exploration and Survey*, p. 37.

[21] Although Captain Stansbury's party, which forded the South Platte a few days later, was composed of veteran voyageurs and mountain men, they found the crossing exceedingly arduous. "Both man and beast suffered more from the day's exertion than from any day's march we had yet made." *Exploration and Survey*, 39-40.

Though the south fork is very wide, there was not more than twenty inches of water in the deepest places.

Between the two rivers, above the junction, are thousands of acres of black, sandy soil, on which grew the finest of grasses and also several varieties of cactus, of which the prickly-pear predominated.

We had gained about two thousand feet in altitude since leaving our old camp on the Missouri.

The fourth of July was ushered in by the discharge of our firearms, and, after a thorough cleaning, they were ready for use again.[22]

We made satisfactory progress up the north fork of the Platte, and as a higher altitude was reached the river became very narrow and rapid, and where it cut through high ridges it formed very deep canyons. The animals found excellent grazing, the road was as good as could have been desired, and the weather fine, with hot days and cool nights.

[22] "Early in the morning we fired several rounds, and made as much noise as possible in honor of the day of Independence. We started in the morning and soon passed an encampment where we had the pleasure of beholding the "Star Spangled Banner" floating in the cool breeze. We traveled a few miles farther and passed another camp with two large American flags waving above it." Webster, *Gold Seekers of '49*, 55-56.

All of us enjoyed good health, and, barring anxiety as to the future and the scarcity of game, the daily marches to the most of the company were quite enjoyable.

Chimney Rock, situated as it is on a level plain midway between the north fork of the Platte and the lofty sandhills which border the wide river bottom, is an object of interest to all lovers of the grand in nature. In the clear atmosphere peculiar to that region it can be seen forty miles away. At this distance it looks like a chimney of some great factory. At a distance of fifteen or twenty miles it appears to the eye as a smooth, perpendicular shaft. On arriving in the vicinity of the rock there was found a large, symmetrical mound covering more than an acre of ground and about one hundred feet high, from the center of which the rock reached a height estimated to be one hundred and eighty feet. The rock, being composed of a soft, gray sandstone, was fast wearing away and adding its waste to the mound below. It was fifty or sixty feet in diameter at the base, and carried its size well to the top. Altogether, it was a rough, ragged pile, and struck one as being more grand than beautiful.

Fifteen or twenty miles from Chimney rock we came to a high ridge through which the Platte, in its fight for the right of way, had formed a canyon five or six hundred feet deep, and the rushing waters were still battling with the rocks which had fallen from the canyon's walls.

Fremont was instructed by the Government to explore and survey the Platte River, on his return from the first exploring expedition to the Rocky Mountains, and for that purpose he was provided with an excellent rubber boat, which he transported from St. Louis to the mouth of the Sweetwater, where it was left while he penetrated and explored the Wind River Mountains. In his party were several Canadian voyagers. They were employed because of the fact that they were known to be experienced boatmen and experts in navigating tortuous streams.

On the return of the party to the Sweetwater, the boat was launched and the voyage down the Platte commenced. It was found to be a foaming torrent from the start, and the boatmen were shot down the rocky channel with the speed of a race-horse. After three or four hours of difficult and dangerous boating, without, as yet, meeting with serious accident, they entered this canyon,[23]

[23] Chimney Rock is in western Nebraska, near the point where the Platte leaves the highlands to enter upon the plains. The canyon where Fremont encountered his misfortune is at the junction of the Sweetwater

42

where their boat was completely wrecked, the boatmen barely escaping with their lives. Much other valuable property was also lost, including records and field notes, surveying and astronomical instruments, besides geological and botanical collections, which had been gathered with much labor and great care, and were of almost priceless value.

It would seem to require but little statesmanship for those in authority to sit in a cozy office at Washington and order Fremont to navigate and survey a river of which they knew nothing.

Having made camp early in the afternoon near a spring of cool water which was gushing from the base of a high cliff, we had an opportunity of visiting the sandstone formations at that time called Scotts Bluffs, only a mile or two from camp, and were amply paid for the time spent, for among them, with a little stretch of the imagination, could have been found the counterpart of everything in ancient or modern architecture, and on a most stupendous scale. There seemed to be immense buildings, with terraces, domes,

with the North Platte, near present-day Casper, Wyoming, much farther to the northwest. The author's memory evidently has confused the two distinct localities.

43

turrets and pinnacles, and a bewildering labyrinth of streets, alleys and broad avenues, the whole forming a veritable city done in soft sandstone.

Where the wind had full sweep, sand-dunes were formed, the outlines and artistic curves of which were very interesting; and the innumerable scales of mica mixed with the sand glistened in the sunlight and added beauty to the scene.

In the clear atmosphere of that locality one is easily deceived as to heights and measurements, and we indulged in much wild guessing relative to the height of some of the vertical walls of the larger formations, which were probably from three to five hundred feet high.

I doubt whether there could be found a cleaner spot in the world, for there was not a trace of vegetation to be seen, and the point visited by us was as clean as pure gray sand could make it.

Ash Creek, a tributary to the Platte, passes through a deep canyon which the road crossed by a steep and difficult trail. Making a noon halt in the narrow valley, four of us, including the Doctor, obtained leave of absence for an hour to give us an opportunity to examine the formation of this wonderful water-course.

The General informed us that the shady nooks along the creek were favorite retreats for deer in the heat of the day, and advised us to carry our guns without covers and ready for immediate use.

After a half-mile or more of climbing and winding among rocks, we found on the east side of the creek a perpendicular wall of soft sandstone about four hundred feet high, in which deep caverns had been worn by the action of water on the more friable portions of the rock. The bank on the west side at this point was quite sloping, while shrubs were growing wherever their roots could obtain a foothold. We halted in the shade of the rock wall, and, while deeply interested in surrounding objects, were startled by a peculiar rushing sound from up the creek which seemed to be drawing nearer. We first thought of mounted Indians, but before we had time to take the second thought six deer, with a very large buck in the lead, were within fifty feet of us, with nothing intervening except low, scrubby bushes. On seeing us, they changed their course and started up the opposite slope, when our four guns, heavily charged with buckshot, were all fired at once, and the old buck came tumbling down the steep bank almost to our feet, while we were surprised and dumbfounded at seeing the other five deer scamper off up the hill quite unhurt. In dressing the game we noticed that its hide was completely riddled with buckshot, and on consulting together we found that in our hurry and excitement all had fired at that tough old buck and let the young and tender meat go scot-free.

Chapter 4

Hunting Buffalo—Chased by Indians—The Tables
Turned—Buffalo Hunters Unhorsed—Wild Sage—
Rocky Hills—Rough Roads—Throwing Away Tents
and Tools—Rock Independence—Devil's Gate—A
New Departure.

BENJAMIN SNOW, an excellent shot
and a persistent hunter, was off for
the hills long before daylight on a still-
hunt for buffalo. Before our train was ready
for the road, he returned and reported the
capture of a fine cow only a short distance
away. My mess was detailed to go with
Snow and secure the meat. There were sev-
en of us in the party; and, in addition to our
riding animals, we took along four pack-
mules with game pouches, having had orders
to take the meat to our noon halting place.

A mile up the road and a short distance
into the hills brought us to the game. We
were but a short time divesting our prize of
its jacket and packing everything eatable on
the mules, being anxious to overtake our
train as soon as possible, for fear of being cut
off from the company by the hostile Sioux
Indians.

Turner, one of our party, was detailed to
hold the horses and keep a sharp lookout, as

47

we always had done when in detached parties. When we were ready to leave, Turner, who was posted on a small hillock, called our attention to a number of moving objects some distance back in the sandhills. He had noticed them for some time, but, thinking they might be buffaloes, had the good judgment to say nothing about the matter until the mules were securely packed. A hasty observation convinced us that an army of mounted Indians were coming toward us as fast as their ponies could bring them. They were, perhaps, a half-mile away, but, being enveloped in a cloud of dust, it was hard to estimate their number, but we thought there were at least three hundred of them.

We mounted our horses at once and forced the pack-mules to their best pace, being anxious to get from the hills into the river bottom before being overtaken by the three hundred Sioux warriors. The main road up the river at this point lay along the bluffs, and we thought our train would not be far in advance of the point where we should strike it. Before we were quite out of the hills, the Indians announced their presence by yelling like a pack of devils, which frightened the horses and was the means of increasing their speed, though the pack-mules did not seem to be at all impressed with the importance

48

of the occasion; but, by the vigorous use of the ramrods from our guns, we held them to time, kept them in the lead and saved the beef.

After such observations in the rear as we were able to make, we became satisfied that the whole three hundred Indians were coming down on us like a whirlwind. They were but a short distance in our rear when we reached the valley, but here we had the good fortune to find ourselves within forty rods of six of our men, who had been detained by re-packing their mules.

Being in the near vicinity of six well-armed comrades and having a good view of our train slowly moving up the valley but a short distance away, gave us much courage; but what put courage in us took it out of the Indians.

Having recovered from our fright and seeing the Indians hesitating, we wheeled around and brought our guns to bear for fight, but they took the back track in good earnest. Whether they would have harmed us had they gotten hold of us they knew best, of course, but we had no disposition to test the matter.

When we became the pursuers and the Indians the pursued, their numbers seemed to have diminished amazingly, for we could count only about fifteen Indians. Whatever

became of the other two hundred and eighty-
five I never knew. The General said he
would wager a beaver tail that there had not
been over a dozen Indians within ten miles
of us; but, of course, we knew better.[24]

On July 8th I had an opportunity of grati-
fying my desire to capture at least one buffalo, for I was then one of the hunters. Exchanging my Spanish saddle-mule for a horse
said to be a leader in the chase, we were off
before sunrise, and in a short time sighted a

---

[24] This stirring tale provides an excellent illustration
of the vicissitudes of a tenderfoot on the plains. Webster, describing what seems to be the same incident
(which he ascribes to June 30) relates: "One of our company killed a buffalo this afternoon, and after we had
camped, Joseph B. Gage, with two or three others, with
mules went back to bring in the meat; but before they
had arrived at the place where it was slain they saw a
band of Indians riding toward them, and they became
frightened and returned to camp with all possible speed.

"The next morning a party of Sioux Indians came
into our camp and desired the doctor should give them
some medicine, stating that their camp was on the
opposite side of the Platte, and that the small pox was
raging among them.

"They were perfectly friendly and said they had no
intention of frightening our men away from the buffalo
meat, but that they wished to talk with them and get
some medicine; and also stated that they made all the
friendly signs that they could think of to have them
stop. The doctor supplied them with medicine and they
left our camp." *Gold Seekers of '49*, 54.

large herd of buffaloes quietly grazing on the river bottom. They were estimated to be four miles away, but in the clear atmosphere of that locality they seemed much nearer. We managed to keep out of their sight until within a mile of them, when they threw up their heads and were soon in rapid motion for the hills. We thought to cut them off by taking advantage of the ground, but they beat us to the bluffs and for a short time were out of sight in a perfect labyrinth of low sandhills, among which they scattered in all directions. It would have been useless to attempt to estimate the number of animals in the herd, for they occupied three or four miles of the river bottom, yet it seemed but a few minutes from the time those nearest us became aware of our presence until every buffalo had gained the bluffs and was lost to view. Our horses became excited and did their best to overtake the fleeing herd. Each hunter selected his route and we were soon out of sight of one another.

An immense cloud of dust hung over the landscape and a buffalo could hardly be distinguished thirty yards away, while numerous washouts, or gullies, made rapid riding both difficult and dangerous.

Back in the hills a mile or two I found myself within twenty yards of the game, and, raising my gun, I fired at the nearest buffalo. The animal didn't fall, but I did. At the report of the gun my horse (not being accustomed to fire-arms) became terribly frightened and changed his course very suddenly, leaving me in a heap on the hard, gravelly earth.

The fall resulted in my being considerably bruised and shaken up, but not otherwise injured. My clothing received some gaping rents, while my canteen was crushed into a shapeless mass and completely ruined. I was pleased, however, to find that my gun had passed through the ordeal without material injury.

The frightened horse took the back track at once, carrying with him my ammunition and small arms, and leaving me with an empty gun to get out of the hills as best I could. Slowly and sorrowfully I walked back to the valley, where I found my horse and joined the other hunters, and thus ended my first and last buffalo hunt.

Here I learned that not a buffalo had been taken from that vast herd, and that two other hunters, as well as myself, had been unhorsed in the grand chase. This ended buffalo hunting on horseback by our party, and we understood what the General meant when he told us at starting out, that with our limited experience and want of trained horses we would be more likely to return from the chase with broken heads than a dead buffalo.

The outcome of this exploit was very disappointing, but, as the prospect of adventure was a great incentive to our crossing the plains, we had no right to complain when finding some things quite disagreeable.

Early in the morning of July 20th we bade a final adieu to the Platte, and, after a long day's march across a dry region, struck the Sweetwater river an hour or two after dark, at a point about one thousand miles from the frontier and seven thousand feet above the level of the sea.[25]

The Sweetwater is a tributary of the Platte, taking its rise in the neighboring mountains where it is fed by melting snow. Its clear, cool water, which was highly appreciated by

---

[25] Webster presents an interesting picture of conditions at Fort Laramie where a three-day halt (July 8-11) was made. The camping grounds near the fort were "literally covered with wagon irons, clothing, beans, bacon, pork and provisions of almost all kinds, which have been left by the advance immigration to lighten their loads and facilitate their speed." Here, too, the Boston party abandoned the trunks which they had carried mule-back for 700 miles, and whose burden had done much to wear down the mules and ruin their backs. At the Sweetwater, dates given by Webster and by Shaw again coincide.

53

our party after having so long used the
turbid waters of the Platte, and the broad
valley which afforded splendid grazing for
our animals, with large quantities of drift-
wood which furnished fuel for cooking,
and the grand view of distant mountains,
besides other interesting objects near by,
combined to make it a camping place at
which we would have liked to remain for
a week.

The country traversed for the preceding
two weeks was rough and rugged. After
crossing the north fork of the Platte, we had
long stretches of dry, barren plains, vast
fields of wild sage, scraggy hills, deep and
rocky ravines, and miles of volcanic rocks
and ashes. The dust from the ashes was very
annoying to both man and beast. Nearly all
of the men had their lips covered with court-
plaster, while their inflamed noses and eyes
showed the effects of the vicious alkaline
dust.

We lost two mules in crossing the north
fork of the Platte, besides three which became exhausted and were left in the barren
hills. It seemed that we were out of the
range of the buffalo, and, though a number
of deer taken along the water-courses added
something to our bill of fare, we drew largely
on our regular supplies.

Wild sage (artemisia) is a small shrub from one to six feet high. It is found from the British possessions on the north to Mexico on the south. It delights in dry, sandy plains and gravelly hillsides, but is shy of river bottoms and rich soils. In color it resembles the common garden sage, and exhales an agreeable odor. It furnished travelers with the means of cooking when no other fuel could be had. It also relieved the desert country of much of its monotony.

On striking the steep and rocky hills, nearly all wagon companies found their wagons overloaded, and, in order to lighten them, such property as they could best spare was left along the road. On our march through the foothills we passed many abandoned wagons, also chains, ropes, saddles, shovels, spades, picks, gold-washers, crow-bars, and a complete outfit for a saw-mill.

As our pack-mules were losing flesh and showing signs of failure, in order to relieve them our tents were thrown aside as surplus plunder, and we slept in the open air. Many other useless articles were left at different points. A large auger, with a very elaborate extension stem, with which we had intended to prospect the lower regions to any desired depth for the yellow metal, was left in the foothills, and a lot of sheet-iron gold-washers, made for the purpose of separating large quantities of gold from the shining sands, found a resting place on the Platte River. Either of the above would have been about as useful in a gold mine as a Texas steer in a china shop.[26]

Rock Independence was near our camp. The granite pile, being isolated and arising from a level plain, is a landmark of enormous proportions and quite worthy to stand as a sentinel over the mountain peaks which are to be seen from its summit. It is nineteen hundred and fifty feet long and one hundred and twenty feet high, occupying twenty-one acres of ground; yet it is only one of the wonders, and quite in keeping with the immensity of objects to be found in that local-

[26] One of the articles whose abandonment Webster records was a "filter," weighing 30 pounds. As far back as Fort Kearney, on June 18, when the Company was inspecting the packs with a view of trying to lighten them, the filter, along with heavy spades, picks, and other articles, came under review. However useful these might prove to be in the mines, some of the Company deemed it impractical "to pack them 2000 miles on the sore backs of mules." Others, however, bitterly opposed the proposal to discard them. Now, a month later, Carlton, on whose mule the filter was packed, and who had several times urged that it be discarded, quietly hid it in a thicket, telling only two or three of the men whom he knew to be sympathetic. *Gold Seekers of '49*, 49 and 61.

ity. Although having been surfeited with rocks for several days, we spent considerable time and enthusiasm in viewing the monster, which looked like it might be a mammoth egg half buried in the earth.

Two or three miles from our camp was the Devil's Gate, where the Sweetwater cut through a granite ridge.[27] The length of the canyon is about twelve hundred feet and the width eighty feet, while the walls of solid rock were over four hundred feet high and appeared to be vertical, but this illusion was dispelled when, after climbing to the summit of the ridge, none of our party of four persons succeeded in throwing a stone across the yawning chasm.

Our camp was near the entrance of the famous South Pass through the Rocky Mountains, the road to which led in a southwest direction for about one hundred and forty miles to the summit, and then about the same distance in a northwest course to a point about due west.

On July 21st we remained in camp and were occupied in washing, mending our cloth-

[27] Independence Rock and the Devil's Gate, noted by almost all diarists of travel over the Oregon Trail, are near the southwestern corner of Natrona County, Wyoming. According to Webster, the Devil's Gate was passed on July 25.

ing and repairing our packs and saddles. While sitting around a bright campfire at the close of the day, the General informed us that he intended to leave the traveled road and take us through the Wind River Mountains, and strike the road on the other side of the main range, where it enters the Great Basin.[28] We were not only surprised and delighted, but heartily endorsed the arrange-

[28] The Wind River Mountains, into which the party was about to plunge, contain some of the roughest terrain and highest peaks in the United States. From South Pass, the Oregon Trail led southwesterly (not northwest, as stated by Shaw) to Fort Bridger, midway between present-day Granger and Evanston in the southwestern corner of Wyoming. From Fort Bridger the Oregon Trail turned north-westward to Soda Springs and Fort Hall. The southward loop made by the digression to Fort Bridger was avoided by many of the emigrants by following the Greenwood, or Sublette, Cut-off, between South Pass and Bear River. This had been discovered by Caleb Greenwood, and more properly should have borne his name. It ran westwardly from South Pass to the Bear River at a point about 60 miles above Soda Springs, where it rejoined the main trail coming from Fort Bridger. It was some 50 miles shorter than the Fort Bridger route, but much of the country traversed by it was a dry desert, while the longer route was well-watered. Shaw's party ignored both routes to turn northward into the Wind River Mountains and follow a trail, passable only by mule back, which led from the vicinity of Mount Fremont westward to Fort Hall, lying a considerable distance to the northward of the main Sublette Cut-off.

ment, as we felt assured that while on the short cut we would find an abundance of water, grass, fuel and game. We were to make the trip by easy marches, with the view of recruiting our animals and adding something to our stock of provisions.

Chapter 5

The Best Hunter—Venison in an Oak Tree—A Change
of Wind—Uncle Ben and Party Lost—Mountain
Wolves—Crossing the Water-Shed—Game in Abundance—Extra Guard Duty—A Mountain Park—
Hunting Bear, Bighorn and Beaver.

OUR hunter, Benjamin Snow, had
spent the greater part of twenty
years of his life in hunting and
trapping in the White mountains and forests
of Maine. Loaded down with a rifle, two
vicious-looking pistols, and a large knife, he
could cover more ground in a given time than
any mule in our outfit. He never hunted on
horseback, claiming that he could secure
more game by still-hunting than any ten
mounted men, and no one could gainsay the
fact.

Uncle Ben was about forty years of age,
nearly six feet high, weighed one hundred
and eighty pounds and built for heavy service from the ground up. He could neither
read nor write, yet he possessed a lot of real
practical common sense. Dressed in a gray
suit, with his unshaven face, long hair and
wide-visored, close-fitting cap, he was an
odd-looking character. He was of a kind and
amiable disposition, very companionable,

and the narratives of his hunting exploits
rendered him a welcome guest around our
campfires. Some of his adventures when
buffalo hunting on the plains are worthy of
mention.

While we were among the hills on the
upper waters of the Platte, one morning
about daylight, Uncle Ben mounted his mule
and started west along the traveled road.
Our train, having made about fifteen miles,
halted for dinner on a small water-course,
where, along the narrow, deep bottoms, were
growing isolated patches of shrubs and
dwarfed trees. Near the crossing, picketed
in a grass plat, we found Uncle Ben's mule,
and near by, hanging from the branch of a
small tree, was the carcass of a fine deer,
from which steaks had been cut, while a
smouldered campfire told where our hunter
had cooked his dinner. A stake about four
feet long was noticed in a conspicuous place,
and in the split top, at right angles with the
upright, had been placed a small stick, with
the sharpened end pointing west.

After cooking and eating the venison for
dinner, we took in Uncle Ben's mule and
pushed on, encamping about dusk in a small
valley, which afforded but little grass and a
meager supply of water. Here we found Uncle Ben. He had killed a large buffalo, about

four miles away, and was waiting for help to
bring in the meat. There was no time to
lose, for it was already a question as to who
should secure the game, ourselves or the
wolves. Hastily watering our horses, filling
our canteens and snatching the game-pouch-
es and beef-saw, ten of us, all mounted, were
soon following Uncle Ben's lead over the hills.
Darkness was coming on apace, a cold wind
had sprung up from the west, angry-looking
clouds were floating over mountain tops, and
there was every indication of a cold and
cheerless night.

Owing to the darkness and sameness of
everything around us, there was some difficulty in locating the game; but we found it,
picketed the animals in the best grass,
dressed the beef, and from it cooked and ate
our supper, after which we packed up and
were off for the camp. It was very dark, and
the wind, which increased in violence, was accompanied with dashes of rain. A sudden
fall in temperature also added much to our
discomfort. Shaping our course by the wind,
which we still thought to be coming from the
west, we plodded on; but, after traveling
four or five hours and finding no camp, the
conviction forced itself upon us that on a
very dark and gloomy night we were lost in
a wilderness. Finding ourselves in a valley,

at the base of a high and rocky ridge which was too steep for horses to climb, we ascended it on foot, but could see nothing of the fire which the boys in camp had promised to keep burning. We then discharged six guns in a volley, but could hear no responsive sound. It being past midnight, we returned to the valley, picketed the animals, selected a guard by drawing lots, posted the victim, and resigned ourselves to fate.

The wind was sweeping down the valley at a furious rate, and, as we could find no shelter from its force, we decided to build a windbreak from the mass of loose rocks at the foot of the hill; but the task had hardly been commenced when some one suggested that it was a good place for rattlesnakes, and moving the rocks might disturb them. We abandoned the scheme at once. Having no fuel with which to make a fire, and being frequently treated to squalls of snow and hail, together with the mournful howling of wolves which had scented our meat, we passed a miserable night.

At the dawn of day we again ascended the hill, which proved to be one of the highest in the vicinity, but we could not recognize any landmarks. The storm had spent its fury and through rifts in the clouds could be seen clear sky, and we were then able to locate the

cardinal points, by which it was discovered
that the wind was blowing from the north,
and our ignorance of the change was the
cause of all our misery. Instead of traveling
south, as we should have done, we had taken
a due westerly course, keeping parallel with
the road and finally finding ourselves about
eight miles nearer California than we cared
to be that morning.

An hour's travel in a southerly direction
brought us to the road, where, knowing that
the company would not break camp until we
were heard from, one of our party was selected
by lot to go and inform the company of our
safety. But a few minutes elapsed before the
one chosen set out on his mission, after which
we cooked and ate breakfast from the meat
that had caused us so much trouble. Without waiting for the arrival of the company,
we started west along the road, continuing
until near noon, when we found water and
halted, being joined by the company soon
afterwards.

At another time Uncle Ben had killed a
buffalo, two or three miles off the road,
but failed to get into camp and report the
fact before night, and, as there were some
doubts about finding the game in the darkness it was left till daylight next morning,
when eight men went out to where the

game was left, but they found nothing except a part of the skin and the larger bones, the wolves having devoured every vestige of the meat.

The large mountain wolves prowled around our camp every night and treated us to the most unearthly, lonesome and homesick music that could be imagined. The only thing that would stop their infernal noise was the report of a gun, and then for only a few minutes. The cowardly brutes never came within reach of our muzzle-loaders in the daytime and were rarely seen at night.

Near nightfall on July 29th, we encamped on the Little Sandy river, a tributary of the Colorado. We had passed the divide and were on the waters that found their way to the Pacific Ocean.[29] We were under the necessity of traveling at a very moderate gait and leading our mules single file, as the trail through rocky gorges and along steep hillsides allowed the passage of only one animal at a time, consequently we made the distance

[29] The "divide" was the famous South Pass. In this paragraph Shaw telescopes the journey from the Sweetwater to the Little Sandy with the subsequent days of travel through the Wind River Mountains. Instead of eight days travel of 110 miles, the distance from the Sweetwater to the Little Sandy was thirteen miles, made in the single day of August 2. *Gold Seekers of '49*, 66.

of only one hundred and ten miles from the Sweetwater in eight days.

We found in the mountains all the requisites of camp life in abundance. Game was plentiful and readily taken, though we had made no attempts as yet to prepare meat for future use. Out stock of bread being nearly exhausted, we were restricted to a purely animal diet and lived on the flesh of the deer, antelope, elk, bighorn, beaver and jack-rabbit.

Beavers along Little Sandy were quite numerous, and wherever there were trees near the banks we found traces of their work. We saw trees one foot through which had been cut down with their teeth.

We were crossing the highest mountains in the Wind River range, and the most of us enjoyed the immensity of that elevated region. We met no Indians after leaving the Sweetwater, but while traversing the territory of the Blackfeet (a jealous and warlike people) the nightwatch was doubled. Twelve men were assigned their stations at sunset and relieved at midnight by twelve others, who remained on their beats until sunrise the next morning. As we were never troubled with insomnia, this extra guard duty was a little trying. As an additional precaution, we placed a sentinel on a high point during our noon halts to give warning of the approach of Indians and watch for game. Volunteers were never lacking for that service, for when armed with the Doctor's field-glass (as was usually the case) they had opportunities which few could hope to enjoy.

The General was anxious to meet some of the Blackfeet, for in former years he had been well acquainted with many of their hunters, and felt confident that a renewal of the old acquaintance would be a sure guarantee of good treatment by the hunters of the tribe as long as we remained in their territory.

Our men at this time, notwithstanding the animal diet, were all enjoying excellent health, and, although we slept in the open air with no covering but our blankets to protect us from the frosty atmosphere, not a cold had been contracted and no complaints were heard from any one.

On July 30th the advance guard was off early looking for a passage through the next range, for we seemed to be in a deep hole and surrounded by rugged mountains and conical peaks. We traveled up the Little Sandy in a northwest course for five or six miles, where we struck a tributary of the river, and up this stream, in a westerly course by a difficult and dangerous trail we toiled until about

2 p. m., when we were rewarded by striking a fine mountain park in which to halt for dinner.[30]

In the little valley of fifteen or twenty acres, nestling between mountain peaks, we found everything needed for our comfort. Even the deer, which furnished the meat for our dinner, was captured on the spot by the hunters who were in advance of our train. The valley was pronounced the most picturesque mountain park yet seen, and many of our party would have liked to camp there for a day. There was no timber within view except small evergreens and thickets of service-berry bushes.

The brooklet along which we rested was coursing through a modest little canyon, twenty feet deep in some places, and at one point not more than four or five feet across the top. A small field of snow on the north side of a mountain peak furnished water for a beautiful little cascade, which was leaping from a shelf of solid rock, with a perpendicular fall of twenty-five or thirty feet, which, with its crystal waters shimmering in the sunlight, formed a scene of rare beauty.

[30] Webster's journal shows that the mountains were entered on August 9, after crossing Green River and ascending an eastward flowing tributary for fifteen miles.

About two hours were spent in that mountain retreat, which proved to be a fine field for students in geology, while in these little valleys, with rare plants in brilliant bloom, the botanist loves to linger.

While at our halt, two bears were sighted by the lookout among the berry bushes, in a gorge not far from camp. Twenty armed men, with their dinners half eaten, followed them for more than an hour, but the bears got away without a scratch; not so the men, for they returned with rent clothing and many small wounds, resulting from forcing their way through the brush.

We worked our way down the west side of the ridge, and some time after dark formed a camp on the west side of the Big Sandy River, where, being well supplied with grass, fuel and venison, the fatigues of the day were forgotten in refreshing sleep, of which he who has never led a pair of stubborn mules across the Rocky Mountains, with wild game as his only food, knows nothing.

Chapter 6

EARLY in the morning on the last day of
July, we left Big Sandy for a climb
over the high mountain ridge which lay
to the west. As the rising sun lighted up the
steep slopes and frowning cliffs, it looked as
though neither man nor beast would ever be
able to scale its lofty heights; but with hard
work and by a very circuitous trail we reached
the summit a little past noon and partook of
our lunch of cold boiled venison, while at the
same time we enjoyed scenery of rare beauty
and awful grandeur. From this elevated
point Fremont's Peak and adjacent mountains, which lay in a northwest direction,
were in plain view, enabling us to realize, to
some extent, the immensity of the surroundings.[31] A small lake, which seemed to be in

[31] The emigrants were in the midst of some of the
roughest country in North America. Several of the
adjacent peaks rise to a distance of almost 14,000 feet.
Fremont supposed, although mistakenly, that the one

a deep rent a little south of us, looked like a
mirror lost in a wilderness. The pass down
the west side of the mountain proved to be
very difficult and, in places, quite dangerous;
yet we found ourselves at dark encamped at
the foot of the mountain in one of the most
beautiful of little parks. A portion of the
way down was along the brink of a deep canyon, where a false step meant a tumble of
many hundred feet.[32] The medicine chest and
ammunition were carried down by the men,
while our animals were all safely landed in the
valley, and the much-abused mule was given
credit for being sure-footed and cool-headed.

Our march for that day was very fatiguing, though interesting, and we gained but a
few miles on our journey, which prompted
some of the boys to ask if it was one of the
General's easy marches.

Climbing mountains proved to be hard
work and sometimes disappointing, for fre-

to which his name was given was the highest in the
United States.

[32] Webster wrote on August 11: "We passed over
places today on the sides of mountains along Indian
trails which were about one foot wide, on both side of
which were steeps, almost perpendicular, for hundreds
of feet on the one side up and on the other down; and in
many places, should a horse or mule make a mistake,
they would be precipitated to the bottom." *Gold
Seekers of '49*, 69-70.

quently, after working our way to a point thought to be the summit of a high ridge, it was found that we had only ascended a foothill, and that rocky benches and often deep gullies, which were difficult to cross, intervened between us and the summit we were aiming to reach, but in cases of that kind we anticipated much pleasure from standing on the loftier pile and viewing the landscape.

These mountains seemed to afford favorite retreats for numerous bears, and, though our hunters had very poor success in capturing them, we saw signs of them everywhere. They were fond of a species of wild cherry which was growing on small trees from six to twelve feet high, but their favorite food seemed to be the service-berry, and in order to more readily gather the little dainties they broke down trees which were from two to three inches through, and from their roots sprouts sprang up and bore fruit after a year or two. In the sunny ravines and gulches impenetrable thickets were thus formed, which, with the rough and rocky nature of the country, afforded perfect cover for bears and other animals, but made it almost impossible and sometimes quite dangerous for hunters to beat through the mountain jungles. The nights in that elevated region were uncom-

VIEW OF THE WIND RIVER MOUNTAINS
Reproduced from John C. Fremont's Report of his Expedition of 1842

fortably cold, and ice formed wherever there was still water.

Two mountain sheep and a fine deer were brought into camp early on the morning of August 1st. We frequently saw flocks of the mountain sheep looking down on us from the cliffs, but when frightened they would bound away and again make their appearance from some higher point. Curiosity often got the better of their discretion, however, and they sometimes ventured within reach of the deadly rifle; but we never saw them plunging over high and perpendicular cliffs, alighting on their heads, as some writers would have us believe.

A high mountain wall to the west of us seemed to bid defiance to our further progress, but soon after starting out we had the good fortune to strike a winding Indian trail, which afforded us an easy passage to the summit, where we halted for dinner. Large fields of snow were seen on the north side of the mountain peaks and slopes. In passing across small bodies of hard-crusted, dust-colored snow, it would hardly be noticed were it not for the grating sound under the feet, the uniform surface and the absence of rocks.

We saw many small lakes at different levels, some of them several hundred feet above

73

others. They were in deep depressions and surrounded by high, craggy cliffs. Undoubtedly they were well stocked with fish, but the want of time and the difficulty of descending to their level prevented us from testing the matter.

We found an abundant supply of water of crystal purity all through the mountains. In addition to numerous springs whose waters were ice-cold, nearly every depression in the hills sent down a small stream, which, in the after part of the day, was flushed with melting snow. The most beautiful little cascades were seen leaping high, perpendicular cliffs, and then plunging into limpid pools and hurrying on to lower levels. In the morning, the supply of snow-water being cut off by the low temperature during the night, the small streams presented a very modest appearance, as they afforded but little water.

Nothing added more to the cheerfulness, comfort, and romance of our journey than good campfires on cool nights, and wherever fuel was found plentiful we used it without stint; though, on dark nights bright fires in deep, narrow valleys, surrounded by mammoth rocks and steep hillsides, formed a weird scene, giving us a realizing sense of our complete isolation from the civilized world and reminding us of the fact of our being in

74

the heart of a vast mountain wilderness, surrounded by wild beasts and wilder Indians. It often produced a sense of loneliness, thoughts of home and friends, and the comforts of civilization.

Having gradually gained in altitude, we experienced no ill effects from the rarified atmosphere when camping ten thousand feet above the level of the sea. From this elevated point can be seen the hills where are found the head waters of four great rivers, namely, Columbia, Missouri, Colorado, and the Platte, which proves this locality to be the summit of Uncle Sam's vast possessions.

The trail which we followed up the mountain promised us an easy descent to the valley to the west, but before we were ready to set out sixteen Blackfeet Indian hunters made their appearance. They came up the trail from the west and were on their way to the Big Sandy for the purpose of hunting game and drying meat. They walked boldly into our camp, saluting us with many a "how-how." They were surprised when the General saluted them in their own tongue, and two of them recognized him at once. The trio seated themselves on the ground and held a long talk, while the balance of them were making a thorough examination of our effects. Supposing them to be arrant thieves

75

(as all Indians were reputed to be) our baggage was closely watched.

A number of these Indians were armed with fairly good guns of an old pattern, of which they had taken the best of care. They were very anxious to trade for ammunition, but, as they possessed nothing which would be useful to us, we presented them with small quantities of powder and lead, with which they were highly pleased. The Indians seemed proud of their long bows and were fond of exhibiting them. They were of excellent workmanship, the brittle red cedar of which they were made being heavily re-enforced by a tough animal sinew, which was laid on with marvelous skill, giving them phenomenal strength. Their arrows were long and slender, neatly feathered and barbed with flints identical in material and shape with those found in our own locality. Their skill in the use of the bow and arrow was wonderful, for they not only made excellent hits at a stationary target, but a hat, being thrown high in the air for one of them to shoot at, came down punctured with two holes, while the owner seemed thankful that his head was not in the hat when the arrow pierced it.

The General learned from these Indians that the trail which we had followed since morning would lead us through the mountains to the head waters of Lewis Fork of Columbia River,[33] near the northern rim of the Great Basin, and that we would pass the village to which these Indians belonged and where the chief of the tribe had his residence. The General was desirous of seeing the chief and obtaining his permission to make an extended hunt in some favorable locality in his territory, where we could prepare meat for future use. Our guests, after having tobacco and a few trinkets distributed among them, took their departure east, while we started west.

We found it no easy matter to follow an Indian foot-trail down the steep mountainside with pack-mules. We were forced, at times, to leave the trail and select a better

[33] The Snake River. Webster records (without mention of the Indians) that Captain Thing admitted he was lost, and thought the party had come too far north of the trail he had followed eleven years earlier. On August 12 a dispute arose, one faction of the emigrants favoring still to follow Thing as guide, while the majority voted to follow down a little stream which was thought to flow to the valley of the Bear. This was done, and a 22-mile journey brought the party back to the Oregon Trail near the mouth of Smith's Fork of the Bear. The disgusted emigrants, who had wandered 12 days in the mountains, derisively christened this route "Thing's Cut-off." *Gold Seekers of '49,* 70-71.

passage, as our mules could not be persuaded to descend some of the steep, rocky slopes. On reaching the base of the mountain we found coursing through a narrow canyon a roaring mountain torrent, about ten feet wide, which, owing to the high banks and rocky channel, we had much difficulty in crossing. With the only spade in our outfit we were over an hour digging down the banks of the stream, which were at this point about twenty feet high and nearly perpendicular, and after filling spaces between large boulders with rocks, we crossed in about two feet of water and formed our camp on the west bank. In order to guard against accidents, we unloaded the most of our mules and carried their packs across the stream by hand. While we were preparing the crossing, one of our pack-mules was crowded over the wall of the canyon, which at that point was sixty or seventy feet high. The large boulders in the bed of the creek caught him, while his pack went whirling down the stream at a lively rate, but was subsequently recovered in a damaged condition. The mule had dumped his pack for the last time.

Our camping place afforded no level ground on which to sleep, the steep mountains crowding down to the very brink of the canyon, through which rushed the foaming torrent, and our camp was one of extreme wildness. The evidence of terrible convulsions which surrounded us; the scrubby cedars under which we slept; the mountain slopes, rocks and cliffs, lighted up by the blaze of our campfires; the danger from camping on the very brink of a deep canyon; the mules climbing around among the rocks while cropping the scanty bunch-grass; the odor arising from the sizzling venison; the little strip of sky seen between the mountain tops; the gurgling of the stream and our remoteness from civilization, formed a scene which is indelibly imprinted on the memory.

Our experience with rattlesnakes was unique. As they were seldom found in New England, but few of our party had ever seen one, and, expecting to meet them on the plains, we had a wholesome dread of them. We were under the impression that they were always on the offensive and hunting for prey, and could spring six or eight feet and fasten their fangs in the flesh of their victim, causing death almost instantly. After leaving the frontier we were very cautious and constantly watching for those terrible snakes, but failed to make their acquaintance until reaching the rocky hills on the upper waters of the Platte, where they were quite numerous, and we had excellent opportunities for studying their habits.

One morning at daylight, after camping for a night in a brushy ravine which some time previously had been burned over, it was discovered that one of our horses was very stiff in the fore legs and quite unable to walk, while his breast was badly swollen and in which was found a very small wound emitting a few drops of blood. Of course a snake was accused of being the author of the trouble, and we wondered that the horse was still alive. The Doctor's attention being called to the case, he, after a thorough examination and considerable hard work (assisted by several amateur veterinary surgeons) succeeded in extracting a snag from the horse's breast as large around as a pipestem and about three and a half inches long. The horse recovered from his supposed snakebite and lived to carry his rider to the end of his journey.

After the experience of that morning it was learned that rattlesnakes were not as aggressive as we had supposed, but quite harmless if let alone, and we seemed to care but little for them, though we always thoroughly examined our sleeping ground before spreading our blankets for the night. We were surprised on finding that the six-foot snakes which we had heard so much about had dwindled down to about thirty inches in length, which proved that distance not only lends enchantment to the view, but also adds much to the length of a snake.

We had excellent opportunities for the study of human nature and soon learned the character of the men composing our company, who, as a rule, proved to be moral, industrious, and agreeable, and yet we had among us the prince of cranks. He was a chronic grumbler and nothing ever met his approval. He was always hungry and thirsty, forever tired and sleepy, too indolent to carry wood or water, and too lazy to wash himself or bathe the saddle-galls on his mules. He would lie, cheat, and steal, shirk guard duty whenever he could frame an excuse, and was a regular all-around nuisance. He never looked on the bright side of anything, and had no eye for the beautiful unless it was cooked; he never saw a grand old mountain until he had thumped his head against it, and then cursed because it was in his way. He could never understand how anything was to be gained by coming in contact with so much grandeur and ruggedness. On one occasion as we were about to encamp on the bank of a stream, in alighting from his mule he sprained an ankle. Seating himself on a rock and baring his foot, he called the Doctor, who gave the foot a glance and said, "wash it," and then passed on. After washing his foot the Doctor was again consulted, who ordered him to wash the other foot. He obeyed the order, after which his hurt was properly cared for. At another time, being remonstrated with for abusing his mule, he flew into a passion and threatened to "do up" the whole crowd, when the boys took him to the river, and I will venture the assertion that he never, living or dead, got a more thorough or lively bathing. Such men as he should have been born too late to cross the plains in '49.

Chapter 7

A Mule's Last Tumble—Camp in the "Wash Bowl"—
Wild Onions—A Promiscuous Tangle—A Blackfoot
Village—An Old Warrior—Squaws Cooking Meat in
Baskets—Indian Babies Decorated—Fattening Dogs
for Food—A Sharp Decline in the Berry Market—
Permission to Hunt on Green River.

ON August 2d we resumed our journey long before the sun penetrated
the deep depression in which we had
spent the night. Our winding trail lay along
the steep mountainside, a sputtering stream
rushing through a deep canyon on our right,
with a high rock wall on our left. While
slowly working our way along the steep slope
of what appeared to be an ancient landslide,
a poor, worn-out mule, which was allowed
to follow without being packed, missed his
footing and went tumbling and sliding down
the steep incline, with rocks, gravel and dust
following in his train. His downward course
was arrested by a large boulder, when he recovered his footing and attempted to climb
the hill, but again fell and was last seen as
he pitched over the brink of the canyon,
at the bottom of which he doubtless ended
his earthly career. On reaching the summit a little before noon we halted for dinner

and were much interested in the formation
of the mountain on which we were resting,
and concluded that in some former age it
had been a conical peak, but we found it to
be a level summit of ten or twelve acres in
extent and in an almost exact circle with
well defined outlines. The numerous rocks
of a cubical form scattered over its surface,
many of them of large dimensions, suggested
to our minds vast quarries worked by myth-
ical giants in former ages. Some of the boys
named the point the "City of Rocks," while
those who discovered or imagined the lowest
point on the summit to be in the center
called it the "Camp in the Wash Bowl."

We discovered in several localities in the
mountains a kind of wild onion, which was
used in flavoring soups made of bones and
remnants of meat. After having been so long
deprived of vegetables, they were a welcome
adjunct to our bill of fare. The Doctor pronounced them healthful, in a general way,
and also excellent as a preventative of scurvy,
from which we were liable to suffer when
living on an exclusive flesh diet, and he advised us to use them freely whenever they
could be found. These wild onions were not
very large, but what they lacked in size was
made up in strength. When eating them in
liberal quantities it is very doubtful whether

we would have been cordially received in re-
fined society.

After an hour's halt we resumed our journey, and down towards the foot of the mountain we came to a place where there had been
a dense growth of scrubby cedar trees, but
the most of them having been blown up by
the roots, it took a good deal of hard work to
get through them, they being in a promiscuous tangle.

Late in the afternoon we struck a pleasant
little valley, through which a fine mountain
stream was flowing, and by following its
course we reached the village of the Blackfeet Indians near nightfall. They had selected for their summer camp a beautiful
natural park, which was surrounded by high,
wooded hills, while the grassy little valley,
with its low, scattering oaks, gave it the appearance of an orchard, as often seen among
the hills of New England. As we came
abruptly into their village, the frightened
women, children, and most of the dogs went
scurrying down the creek and were out of
sight in a jiffy. Neither was there a man to
be seen. But the General, calling to them
in their own tongue, brought out from their
wigwams several old men, who were soon on
friendly terms with all of us. The dignified
old Chief welcomed the General in a cordial

and friendly manner, treating him as an old friend and inviting him to his lodge, where they ate, smoked, and talked for many an hour.

The Chief gave us permission to form our camp near his village, and assured us that we need entertain no fears about being molested by his people during our stay, but the General cautioned us to keep a sharp lookout for our property, and gave us to understand that the Blackfeet Indians were never too young nor too old to steal from the white man. A vigilant watch was kept through the night, but, except the hideous howling of the Indian dogs, nothing unusual occurred.

On the morning of August 3d the Indian camp was all astir. We saw no women or children about the village the night before, but that morning they were at home, dogs and all. The Chief visited our camp early, accompanied by two squaws carrying deer skins, which they spread on the ground, forming seats for the General and the members of his mess. The Chief, by special invitation, was to breakfast with the General.

Four other dignified old Indians were strolling around our camp and seemed deeply interested in the preparations for breakfast. They readily accepted an invitation to eat

86

with us, and we fed them from our choicest stores. They ate with ravenous appetites and appeared capable of stowing away a vast amount of food, but never seeming to have quite enough. I hardly think it would be safe to try the "quail-a-day" racket on an old Blackfoot hunter.

One of the superannuated hunters we judged to be very old, though we could ascertain nothing from him or his companions as to the number of his years. He was nearly blind and barely able to walk without help, and he had passed the period when he was as straight as the proverbial Indian of most writers. His companions ministered to his wants with a care that would put to shame many a pale-face brother. He was tall and broad-shouldered, and, if in his prime he possessed skill and bravery in proportion to his noble frame, was surely a warrior to be dreaded. We speculated much among ourselves as to his age, and estimated him to be at least a hundred and twenty; but the Doctor, after an examination of the old man (to which the latter submitted without protest), gave it as his opinion that he was not over eighty-five years of age. This verdict was not very flattering to our judgment; yet, notwithstanding, we pronounced him a regular old mummified specimen.

Here we had an opportunity of seeing Indians at home and to observe their habits. Breakfast being disposed of, the old Indians took us through the village, which was composed of about twenty-five lodges; but, as it was a summer camp, many of the wigwams were temporary affairs, a number of them being made by leaning poles against branches of trees, while skins of wild animals formed the covering. Others were constructed by placing poles in a circle around trees and covering with brush, while, hanging on the body of the trees, in the center of the lodges, there were oval-shape shields about twenty inches long and a half-inch thick. They were made of green buffalo hide, and, to secure the proper thickness, two pieces were skillfully glued together. After being thoroughly dried, they were absolutely arrow-proof. We also noticed spears, six to ten feet long, made of red cedar and barbed with flints. They were perfectly straight and neatly finished. There were also bows, quivers containing arrows, moccasins, belts, and many other articles dear to the heart of an Indian.

The Chief's place of abode was of a different order of architecture, it being constructed of poles about twenty feet long, which were set at an angle, forming a cone about

fifteen feet in diameter at the base. It was
covered with finely-dressed buffalo and deer
skins, which, being artistically ornamented,
gave the Chief's home a very novel and interesting appearance; but we received quite
a shock on noticing the uncomfortable and
filthy condition of the interior. The lodges
and cooking of these Indians were all exceedingly filthy and quite repulsive.

The great number of dogs around camp,
which were of all sizes and ages, struck us
with astonishment. The older ones kept
their distance, but the puppies were continually tumbling about our feet and nipping at
our shoes, while near by we discovered an
enclosure about five feet square, formed of
rocks and covered with poles, in which a
good-sized dog was being fattened for a
feast, but of the importance of the occasion
requiring such a delicacy nothing could be
learned.

We were surprised to hear one of the old
Indians speaking in English. He informed
us that he had sometime previously made a
journey with white trappers down the Columbia River to the Pacific, where he spent
two years and then returned to his tribe. I
think the old heathen made application to
every man in our company for whisky, and,
though he failed to obtain the coveted

article, had excellent success in begging tobacco.

Here we saw the Indian squaws boiling meat in baskets. In my younger days I had heard of this being done, and was at a loss to know how a basket could be made to hold water, but when I saw their filthy method of cooking had filled all the open spaces between the ribs of the basket with dirt, the mystery was explained. Their baskets for cooking purposes were about six or eight inches deep, sixteen to twenty inches in diameter, and almost the exact shape of a large wooden bowl. In front of each lodge a few rocks were arranged, forming a small fireplace, in which fire was burning, while in and around the fire were quite a number of round, smooth stones, about the size of base-balls. The heated stones, which were handled with two sticks the thickness of a lead pencil and about a foot long, were being taken from the fire by the squaws and placed in the boiling baskets, and the sputtering which followed seemed to be highly satisfactory to the operators. One of the old squaws, noticing our interest in the matter, handed me the sticks and motioned for me to go to work. I accepted the challenge, and, after several trials, succeeded in taking a stone from the fire, dropping it in the boiling water with a splash

and burning my hands quite severely. I
made no attempt to repeat the experiment,
while the old squaw laughed at my dismal
failure.

Some of the boys were curious to see an
Indian baby, but the squaws, at first, flatly
refused to show them, when John Turner,
one of our party, who kept in stock a supply
of Indian jewelry, fished from his capacious
pockets a fine string of glittering beads,
which, with a few words from our English-
speaking Indian, was the means of there being offered for exhibition a nude and very
dirty baby, and its neck was at once encir-
cled with the shining baubles; but the mother of the baby intimated that the decoration
was not complete without ear-rings, which
she insisted on having. John proved equal
to the occasion by producing the coveted
articles, while, by this time, several other
squaws were ready to present their papooses
to him for decoration. The children were all
provided with beads, from the infant to
those ten or twelve years of age, and the
squaws were each presented with a dozen
polished brass buttons.

During the excitement that followed the
acquisition of so much wealth, the fires were
suffered to burn low, the baskets ceased to
boil, the dogs were quarreling over the half-

cooked meat which they had stolen from the baskets, while the women and children were gathered in a knot and in a babel of voices discussed the merits of their precious treasures.

Near the Indian camp was a large grove of service-berry bushes, and quite a quantity of the ripe berries had been gathered and dried by the squaws, who were very anxious to exchange them for such articles as our boys had to trade. They offered to give a half-bushel or more of the dried fruit for a darning-needle; but when it was learned that the fruit had been dried on the flesh side of green deer skins spread on the ground, with flies, dirt and dogs around, there was a sharp decline in the berry market. What struck us as being most abundant about the Indian camp was, first, dirt; second, dogs; third, more dirt.

The old Chief was a very dignified and prepossessing Indian, but we thought him quite crafty, when, to give us the privilege of hunting for five days on Green River, he exacted two mules, quite a quantity of tobacco, ammunition, and trinkets, though he proposed to throw in an Indian guide to conduct us to good pasturage and hunting grounds. The old man got all he asked for except the mules, and, judging by his actions, he was satisfied that he had gained the best end of the bargain, and time proved that he had.

After an early dinner we resumed our journey. The Chief detailed the English-speaking Indian to guide us to the hunting ground assigned us. As he was continually boasting of his achievements, honesty, and righteousness, the boys called him St. Brag. The old man mounted one of our mules and led us a long march over a very rough and broken country to Green River. Owing to the distance and difficult trail, it was past midnight before the last of the boys came straggling in.

Chapter 8

The Hunter's Paradise—Drying Venison—Six Indian
Boys—An Object Lesson—A Night Adventure—
Driven Out of Camp—"A Set Up Job"—The Lost
Bear Hunters—"Peg Leg Smith"—Washing on the
Plains—Fate of "Tom Thumb."

AT daylight the next morning it was discovered that we had been conducted
to a delightful spot, where, the river
hills receding, was formed a level, timberless
bottom of two or three hundred acres, thickly
set with the finest grasses. This, together
with the surrounding hills, which were clothed
with timber showing different shades of
green; the little valleys between with their
sparkling brooks; the higher mountains in
the distance; the giant rocks; the clear and
rapid river with its pebbled bed, and the
mammoth cotton woods which lined its
banks, combined to make it a paradise for
the hunter.

St. Brag and about twenty of our men were
off before daylight on a grand hunt. The
balance of our men were set to work erect-
ing flakes on which to dry the meat of any
game that might be secured. Five deer were
brought in before ten o'clock, and the day's
hunting resulted in the capture of thirteen

deer, two beavers and a large number of
jack-rabbits. The meat was cut into thin
strips, placed on the flakes and, with the sun
above and fire and smoke below, soon dried,
when it looked like sole-leather and was
about as tough. Service-berries were found
quite plentiful in the ravines among the hills,
and, with our meat diet, they were highly
relished.

While hunting two or three miles above
our camp we discovered that the river had
cut its way through a high mountain ridge,
forming a canyon with precipitous walls
not less than six hundred feet high, while the
river was rushing down a steep incline among
large boulders with a deafening roar. Owing
to the low stage of water, we were enabled to
explore the entire length of the canyon, where
we enjoyed a scene of majestic grandeur.

While we were cooking supper six Blackfeet Indians came marching down the river
towards our camp. They were leading two
ponies, loaded with Indian trappings and
dried venison. They walked into our camp
without hesitation, unpacked their ponies,
and acted as though they had rights which
we were bound to respect. They were mere
boys, probably from sixteen to twenty years
of age, and a very impertinent, thieving set.
They readily accepted an invitation to take

supper with us, and they ate as though they had been fasting for that special occasion.

Here we had another object lesson in Indian culinary art. St. Brag, with the help of the Indian boys, built a fire and placed on and around it quite a number of stones of different sizes. The heads of several deer, which had been thrown aside, were taken by the old Indian, who, after inserting a stick in the mouth of each, held them over the blazing fire until the hair was completely burned off. The heads, without further preparation, together with two beaver-tails, were neatly wrapped in deer-skin, with the flesh side in, and the whole securely tied with willow twigs. The fire having burned down, the larger stones were placed in a circle, forming a cavity into which the bundle of heads was fitted, and over all was placed the small stones and pebbles which had been heated in the fire. The whole was then covered with coals, ashes, and sand to the depth of five or six inches and left till morning, when, the oven being opened, the deer-heads and beaver-tails were found done to a turn, and from them seven Indians made their breakfast, which they seemed to prefer to our fried venison and stewed service-berries.

The General had arranged an elk hunt for the next day, and Uncle Ben had selected his partners for a deer hunt. We were called by the guards before daylight, and after a hurried breakfast the hunters were off for the hills; the fishermen were strolling up and down the river hunting for deep holes, while the six young Indians were looking through our camp to see what they would best try to steal. The elk hunt for the day proved a failure, and deer hunting was far from satisfactory, as the game seemed to have all run away. The Indians said "too much white man, too much shoot."

Our Indian boys were still with us, and there was no prospect of their leaving. They were living on the fat of our camp and had to be watched continually or they would have stolen everything. They seemed to consider themselves as having license to take whatever they could hide or carry away, and acted accordingly.

We found that after paying for the privilege of hunting for several days in the Blackfoot country, and having as yet taken but little game, we were about to be driven out by six Indians, all mere boys at that. Many of our party believed the whole job was arranged by the old scoundrel of a Chief, in order to rob us of everything.

About 5 o'clock P.M. we were ordered to be ready to resume the journey early next morning, but to give the Indians no indication of our intention; yet it seemed they divined our purpose of breaking camp and were resolved to make the most of their last chance.

We had in our company a big, brawny, good-natured Irishman, who possessed uncommon muscular strength, and on proper occasions never hesitated to use it. He was assigned to special guard duty from midnight to sunrise. While the regular guards were on their beats, surrounding the camp and animals, he, with two others, was detailed to keep the Indian boys from stealing everything in the camp, but in this he had no end of trouble. He caught three of them in the act of taking a blanket from the river, where it had been left for the purpose of washing. A violent struggle ensued, at the end of which our Mike retained one-half of the blanket and the Indian boys the other half. The whole camp was aroused by the tumult, and as it was near morning we commenced preparations to resume our journey. It was learned from the guards that the Indians had taken their ponies outside of the picket line during the night and gone with all their effects. They had also taken with them that half blanket, five or six shoes (mostly odd ones), one of our best saddles, and several cooking utensils. St. Brag was also missing, but when or how he got away nobody knew. We were glad to be done with the Blackfeet, though we looked upon them as a very interesting people and as noble types of the American Indian. They had none of that shriveled and dwarfed appearance which was afterwards found to be characteristic of the Root Diggers of the Great Basin. Occupying, as they did, a section of country abounding in game, together with a variety of wild berries, seeds, and edible roots, their food supply was abundant. They were capable of being the warmest of friends or the most bitter of enemies, as best suited the occasion.

On August 10th we made an early camp on an island in Bear River, the principal tributary of Salt Lake. Here the General had an opportunity of visiting an old friend who lived on this island.[34]

After leaving Green River, whose waters find their way to the Pacific, we crossed sev-

[34] The "old friend" was Peg Leg Smith. Webster's journal shows that the party first reached the Bear near the mouth of Smith's Fork, on August 12, "after having wandered in the mountains for twelve days." On August 13 they descended the river ten miles to the Thomas Fork, and on August 14, after crossing a mountain spur, came again to the river at Peg Leg Smith's establishment.

eral low mountain ranges, which seemed to
have been thrown up in promiscuous masses
without regard to order or system, and which
were found even more difficult to cross than
the higher mountains farther east. We
would sometimes climb to the top of a ridge
to find that the only way to get down was
the way we had just climbed up. Therefore
we were often compelled to retrace our steps,
and on one occasion, after a hard afternoon's
work, pitched our camp for the night in the
same little valley in which we had halted for
dinner.

On the second morning from Green River,
Uncle Ben, with three companions, set out
on a bear hunt. Their continued absence
caused us some uneasiness, but they finally
came in alive, after having been three days
lost in the hills and canyons. They had evidently had a rough time, for their clothing
was in tatters, and they were bruised and
lame from tumbling around among the rocks.
They were quite overjoyed on getting back
into camp, and seemed glad that they were
spared to tell the tale. They were loaded
down with bear meat and blood-curdling accounts of their hair-breadth escapes and
thrilling adventures. The meat was soon disposed of, but the bear stories were treasured
up for the benefit of later generations. Our

quartette of bear hunters became the butt
of many jokes, but they always referred to
the fact that they got the bear and we ate
the meat.

Near our camp on this island lived "Peg
Leg" Smith, a white man who had a unique
history.[35] The General had been well ac-

---

[35] Peg Leg Smith was a noted mountain man, concerning whose adventurous life many tales have been
told. Necessarily, some of them are incapable of verifi-
cation, and the sketch which follows may not be correct
in all of its details.

Thomas L. ("Peg Leg") Smith was born in Garrard
County, Kentucky, in 1801. Impelled by the severity
of his parents, he left home while still in his teens, and
engaged in a variety of adventures on the lower Mississippi and Missouri frontiers. About the year 1824
he crossed the plains to Taos. In 1827 in a fight with
Indians somewhere on the upper Platte his leg was
shattered by a hostile bullet, and since none of his
companions had the skill or assurance to amputate it
he performed the task himself with his hunting knife.
Borne on a litter to the trappers' headquarters, he
there recovered his health, and presently affixed a
hickory stick to the amputated stump of his leg. Thereby he gained the sobriquet of "Peg Leg," by which he is
still commonly known. He claimed to have crossed
the mountains to California in 1829, and about this
time predicted its ultimate settlement by Americans.
After years of trapping, fighting Indians, and living as a
squaw man (in one battle between two bands his horse
ran away into the midst of the foe, upon whom Peg
Leg dealt such lusty blows that after the fight had ended
in victory his grateful allies offered him all the wives he

quainted with him in former times; had
hunted and trapped with him and probably
knew more of his history than any other
white man then living, and from him I gleaned
the following: About the year 1800, Smith
and two other restless and adventurous boys
of uncertain age were trapping on the frontier of the then unknown West, but they
longed for a wider and more romantic field
in which to ply their chosen vocation. They
were ambitious to emulate the veteran trappers of the Rocky Mountains, of whom they

might care to take; he modestly contented himself
with three), in 1848 he settled for a time on Bear River
athwart the trail to Oregon and California, where our
author's party encountered him. In a well-written letter
published in the St. Joseph *Adventure*, May 19, 1848 he
announced that he was building a trading post "for the
purpose of supplying the Oregon emigrants with all
sorts of vegetables"; he would soon have a large farm
in cultivation, and he would pay a liberal price to
emigrants for their broken down cattle.

Apparently during the next year or two he pauperized
himself in extending aid to destitute emigrants, for
which he vainly sought repayment by the California
Legislature. The latter years of his life were passed in
poverty in San Francisco. He died in the City and
County Hospital, October 19, 1866, and was buried in
the potter's field. Biographical sketches of his career
were published in the San Francisco *Daily Alta California*, March 8, 1858 and in the *Evening Bulletin*,
Oct. 26, 1866. See also, E. L. Sabin, *Kit Carson Days
1809-1868* (New York, 1935), index entries.

had heard so much. With their arms, ammunition, beaver traps, and two small mules, on which were packed all their earthly belongings, they set their faces to the West, with nothing less than the Pacific Ocean as their goal. In early winter they found themselves in the Wind River Mountains, and as it was too late in the season to continue their journey to the Pacific (as was their intention) they took up their abode with the Blackfeet Indians, with whom they continued to live for an indefinite length of time. The Crow Indians, having declared war with the Blackfeet, invaded their country, and a terrible battle ensued in which Smith's two companions were killed and himself seriously wounded. Having been shot in the knee with a poisoned arrow, his wound was very dangerous, but he was cared for by the Blackfeet, who, after their remedies and incantations failed to cure the wound, amputated his right leg above the knee, from which he fully recovered. He was then adopted into the tribe, became a full-fledged Blackfoot, and married one of their dusky maidens. His residence was built of sun-dried bricks. Its size was fourteen by twenty feet, with walls six feet high, and was covered with a roof of long strips of bark, while a stone fireplace in one end, with a hole in the roof for the passage of smoke, completed the outfit. The floor was of mother earth, while buffalo and deer-skins were the only furnishings of the room. In this miserable hovel "Peg Leg" Smith had lived for thirty-five years, during which time he had raised a large family of half-breeds. He had the reputation of being the most expert trapper of the Rockies, and from him the young men of his tribe took their first lessons. He seemed to have made no effort to improve himself or his surroundings, nor was there evidence of his having cultivated the soil. The little bottoms along the river, which were extremely rich, had never been polluted by the hand of a white Indian. He lived upon the fruits of the chase and such spontaneous productions as were found in his locality. He was scantily dressed in buckskin and went stumping around on a wooden leg of his own make, while his long hair and smoke-cured face gave him the appearance of being as good an Indian as any of them, but I failed to see that he was any better.

To show that "Peg Leg" Smith was not a myth, the following dispatch from Yuma, Arizona Territory, was published in the Indianapolis *Journal*, July 11, 1895:

"Yuma, A. T., July 10: It is now generally believed that the old mine found near India, on the desert, by the McHaney brothers, is the old "Peg Leg" mine, found by "Peg Leg" Smith and party sixty years ago. The quality of quartz, old workings, human bones, kind of gold, richness of ore and location indicate that it is really the old mine. It is producing from $300 to $1,000 per day in a two-stamp mill. Two million dollars has been offered for the property."

The reader may be curious to know how we did our washing when crossing the plains. We adopted the trappers' system, though we could only practice it when camping on rapid streams of clear water and was managed about as follows: We first secured a pole the length of a fishing rod, but somewhat larger and stronger, and fastened a strong cord five or six feet from the small end and another at the extreme point, then securely tied the loose ends of them to the corners of a blanket to be washed, and to the outer corners of that another blanket, and as many shirts or other garments as we cared to wash. By placing rocks around the rod it could be set at any desired angle; or, if a rod was not to be found, we tied the cords to rocks and sunk them in the proper place, which gave the same results, though this sometimes necessitated deep wading. This outfit was placed in the current of the stream where the water was a foot or more deep, and the different articles floated near the surface, while the water gave them a gentle, undulating motion. Under favorable conditions a washing of this kind was completed in one or two hours. Though we had no facilities for giving our shirts a laundry finish, no Chinaman could more thoroughly wash them. We exercised much care in tying knots and making connections, or we might have been under the necessity of finishing our journey without shirts or blankets.

For several days before leaving our camp at Independence, there was noticed among our animals a mule which was supposed to be about a year old, but very small for that age. Where he came from or how he happened to be with us no one seemed to know. On leaving the frontier he followed us and soon became a general favorite with the boys, for besides his gentle and playful ways, it was found that he could run faster, jump farther and climb higher than any other animal in our outfit. Owing to his diminutive size, he was named Tom Thumb, which was soon abbreviated to Tom. When on the march he formed a habit of stopping by the wayside and appropriating to himself such verdure as suited his taste, after which at his best speed he would rush to the head of the column and take his favorite place near the General's bell-horse, of which he was very fond. When crossing the Wind River Mountains he sometimes had trouble in working his way around the pack-mules which had passed him while grazing. On one occasion early in the day, as we were carefully making our way along a very dangerous trail on a steep, rocky hillside, Tom, in his hurry to pass a number of pack-mules at a point which was barely wide enough for one mule to pass at a time, was crowded over a mass of rocks, six or eight feet high, alighting on a smooth ledge which sloped at an angle of sixty or seventy degrees, and in a twinkling shot down the incline into a small canyon through which a mountain stream was flowing.

To approach the canyon at that point was out of the question, and, had that been possible, we dare not leave the mules we were leading, consequently Tom received no attention, but we supposed it to be the last of him, and during the dinner hour many regrets were expressed over the untimely death of our pet. Judge of our surprise when, after going into camp for the night, Tom came limping in looking for the bell-horse. He was bruised and bleeding from many wounds, and with one ear torn half way off and hanging down over a badly swollen eye, he looked

the picture of despair. His wounds were
dressed and he was kindly cared for, yet he
never fully recovered from the effects of his
adventure, but (limping along) managed to
accompany the bell-horse to the end of the
race.

Chapter 9

NEAR nightfall on August 15th we encamped on Goose Creek, a small tributary to Lewis Fork of the Columbia
River, in the southern part of what is now
the State of Idaho, and about two hundred
miles north of the Great Salt Lake. At the
point where we struck the creek there had
been a regular camping place, and the grass
in that vicinity had all been consumed; but,
by moving up the creek a mile or two, excellent grass and ice-cold spring water were
found, and we tarried there all of the next
day.

The past, present, and future of our undertaking was fully discussed, resulting in a discouraging outlook for everything before us.
Our animals had not received the benefit
from our flank movement that we were led

to expect, for, owing to the rocky and gravelly nature of the steep mountain trails, nearly all of them were barefooted and the feet of many of them had become so worn that they were scarcely able to travel.

We supposed ourselves to be not less than eight hundred miles from the valley of the Sacramento, and, considering the condition of many of the animals, could not expect to reach the end of our journey before the first of October. We were about to cross the Great Basin, which was supposed to be almost destitute of timber and game, and where we might expect to find long stretches of dry, barren plains, without water or grass. The General had never ventured into that mysterious region, and knew nothing about the country we were about to enter, so in that respect could be of no further use to us as guide; but where hundreds of wagons had made their way we, with pack-mules, could follow.

With the exception of a small quantity of dried meat, saved from our Green River hunting camp, we had not to exceed ten pounds of provisions to each man. We had eaten nothing but animal food and berries since leaving the Sweetwater, and for the last fifteen days of our march had not tasted salt, the supply of that article having been exhausted. As we were nearing the starvation point, the above considerations suggested to us a division of the party; and after much deliberation it was decided to select five men from the members of the company to act as pioneers and proceed with all possible dispatch to the nearest point where supplies could be obtained and purchase such stores as they should deem best. They were then to procure pack-saddles, load the supplies on their riding animals, and return (walking) meeting the company as far back on the road as possible. The following were elected as pioneers, viz.: D. K. Knowls, E. S. Perkins, Stephen Forseth, Fred Carpenter, and the writer.[36]

Though regarding the proposed trip a very hazardous undertaking, we commenced at once to make arrangements to start the next morning. We were well aware of the risk of the journey, for, being about to traverse an unexplored desert, our small party would be liable to meet with savage tribes, necessitating eternal vigilance and a con-

[36] Webster, who dates the arrival at Goose Creek as on August 28, states that Calvin S. Fifield and Dr. Haynes were sent in advance to make necessary arrangements for the arrival of the body of the Company in California. It is impossible to reconcile the respective statements of Shaw and Webster at this point.

stant watch, both by day and night, and we also knew that we were liable to suffer with hunger and perhaps die of starvation in a region destitute of game, and which was then almost unknown to man.

We were each provided with two hundred dollars in gold, and, in addition to our guns and a good supply of ammunition, our friends persuaded us to accept hunting knives and revolvers till we were about as well armed as the Indian-killer in a dime novel.

Our five pack-mules, with the packs, were to be taken along by the main company and kept with it, and we were disburdened of all articles not absolutely necessary.

The provisions of our party for the eight-hundred-mile trip consisted of ten pounds of Spanish pinoli (parched corn meal sweetened with sugar) and about three pounds of deer tallow.

As we intended, if possible, to make about forty miles per day, we expected to overtake a great many wagon trains, from which it was hoped we would be able to procure supplies enough to keep us from starving.

It being necessary to have riding animals which could be relied on to make long marches, we were given the privilege of making our own selection from the company's entire outfit; but, being so much attached to the saddle animals which had carried us safely from the frontier, we looked upon them as friends and declined exchanging them for those which would probably be no better. But, acting on the advice of the General, we took along a small, tough, hard-footed pony, giving us an extra in case any of the other animals became footsore or otherwise disabled, and after being led one day's march he followed without further trouble.

Our cooking utensils consisted of one large, badly-battered coffee-pot (which had been picked up along the road) two tin cups, and a large iron spoon.

We received no specific instructions. "Do as you think best and be quick," was the word.

Being one of the five selected for this forlorn-hope, I regretted being under the necessity of leaving my messmate and intimate friend, S. D. Murdough. Having had a mild attack of mountain fever, he was considerably prostrated, and, as there had been little or no improvement in his condition for several days he was becoming discouraged and, I feared, somewhat homesick. As he suffered from cold on chilly nights, I gave him the use of my overcoat, and offered him such advice as I was able to give, also assuring him that we would return in the least possible time with supplies, when he would have food better adapted to his condition. I counseled him to maintain a cheerful spirit and to exercise his will in a fight for his former health and strength; but he parted with me as with a friend whom he never expected to see again. On our return to the company my fears were fully realized, for my friend lay buried in the Humboldt Valley.

After much hand-shaking and many wishes for success, we left the company a little after daylight and crossed the watershed which separates the waters of the Columbia from those of the Great Basin. From the summit of the dividing ridge, with something akin to dread, tinctured with regret, we obtained a distant view of the mysterious and unknown desert which we were about to enter.

After being fifteen hours on the road, we camped on a small creek in the lower foothills of the dividing ridge, near the northern rim of the Great Basin. We had excellent grass for our horses, but water was only to be found in deep pools along the bed of the creek. Many clusters of small willows were growing along the narrow creek bottom. Being very weary after our long march, and not thinking it best to make a fire which might attract Indians, we each stirred about two ounces of pinoli in a pint of cold water and drank the mixture for supper. It proved to be anything but a satisfying food, but as a cathartic it was a decided success.

We were much disturbed and obtained but little sleep during the night, as our horses, from midnight to near daylight, were nervous and excited, and we had hard work to quiet their fears and save them from stampeding. Whether it were Indians or animals prowling around our camp we never knew. It would not do to say that we were frightened, but, as for myself, I felt as though I should have liked to be farther away from those willows.

After our experience of that night with cold water and raw corn meal we had no appetite for breakfast, and at daylight set forth on our first day's march in the Great Basin. Our trail lay to the south, over a very rolling and barren country.

After eight hours' travel we struck a dry creek, where, among the willows, we found a scanty supply of grass for our horses. We were weary, hungry and nearly sick. As we had eaten but little food and having had scarcely any sleep for over thirty hours, we felt pretty sober; but, using our coffee-pot as a camp-kettle and water from our canteens, we made a quantity of pinoli porridge, which, after being thoroughly cooked, proved to be both palatable and nutritious. Steve remarked that "it was surprising to see what an amount of cheerfulness could be extracted from a little hot gruel."

After a short rest we resumed our journey, and late in the afternoon found water, where we remained till midnight and again started out. Soon after daylight we discovered smoke some distance ahead, and supposing it to arise from the campfires of travelers, we became anxious and quickened our pace, while we imagined we could almost see the boys of a wagon train, three or four miles away, cooking their breakfast. We were quite disappointed on finding that what we took to be smoke was steam arising from a hot spring in a deep valley. Near the spring was a number of abandoned wagons and the irons of others which had been burned in making fires, indicating that the place had been a favorite camping ground. We were much pleased at finding smouldered camp-fires and evidences of a wagon train having occupied the valley the night before. The hot spring was of no mean dimensions, the reservoir being about forty feet in diameter and the estimated depth seven or eight feet. The water was as clear as crystal and the bottom of the reservoir, which could be plainly seen, was a mass of sand and pebbles kept in constant motion by the water, which seemed to be forced up over the entire bottom of the pool. The discharge from the spring was not much below the surrounding surface, which was nearly level. The flow was uniform and at the rate of two or three hundred gallons per minute. This overflow formed a small rivulet, which diminished in volume for about two hundred yards, where the water disappeared in a bed of gravel and sand. The water from this spring was not boiling hot, though the motion of the water and steam arising from it gave it that appearance. The hand could be held in the water for the space of two or three seconds. Steve said he could "see no use for so large a boiling pot unless we had more meal."[37]

After a breakfast of hot porridge, we started forth, and before noon, by rapid traveling, overtook the wagon train which had camped in the hot-spring valley the night before. We found this wagon company composed of about thirty-five men, who had started from Missouri with nine wagons and forty head of oxen; but at the time we met

[37] According to Webster the advance party left the camp on Goose Creek on August 27, and must have reached the hot spring on or about August 29. The main party arrived there on August 31.

them they were reduced to five wagons and thirty head of oxen. They seemed to be traveling woefully slow, their oxen being footsore and weary; but the men were in good health and quite cheerful, and while they expected to have reached the end of their journey before that time, yet they had no fears as to the result. We were soon well acquainted and each one had learned something of the other's perils and adventures while on the plains. They had taken but little game along the way, and consequently had drawn heavily on their stores, and were not in condition to sell us supplies; but they gave us a little flour, a few ounces of salt, and a small frying-pan, and in addition to the above a tin plate (a much needed article) was added to our stock of tableware.

After a nooning of two or three hours and a dinner of porridge, supplemented by flap-jacks seasoned with salt, we bade adieu to our kind friends and traveled till past midnight; but, finding no water or grass, we halted for three or four hours, when we resumed our journey and had the good fortune to strike a camping place a little after sunrise, and after a short rest pushed on again. Our road was across a sage desert. As far as the eye could reach nothing could be seen but the blue sky and a wilderness of wild sage. The sun was excessively hot and there was not a breath of air in motion. A profound stillness hovered over the landscape and we seemed to travel in a world of sunshine, silence, and sage. The only living thing seen during the day was a number of horned toads, and on our march of thirty-five miles we found not a drop of water. A little before dark, being weary, hungry, and somewhat discouraged, we selected a camping place in a little valley between two low hills which were clothed with a dense growth of sage. A little strip of grass near by furnished a scanty supply of feed for our animals, and a hole scooped out in a moist spot in the earth kept us from suffering for water. The little valley was not to exceed thirty or forty feet in width between the lines of sage. While gathering fuel to cook our supper, two Digger Indians came slipping through the sage into our camp and took their stations near our fire. In less than five minutes two more made their appearance, and singly and in pairs they continued to come until we had seventeen of them. They were absolutely naked, poor, and hungry, and quite in keeping with the character of the country. The average stature of these Root Diggers was not to exceed five feet, and their weight seventy to ninety pounds. Their faces were pinched and care-worn, while the most abject misery seemed stamped on every feature, and we looked upon them as types of humanity in its lowest form. How they managed to support existence in that miserable country, or why they were there, was an unsolved mystery. They ate everything that afforded the least nourishment—roots, seeds, snakes, insects, and, in short, everything that helped to prolong their miserable lives. They were armed with ugly-looking clubs and very inferior bows, with a meager supply of arrows. We could make nothing out of their language, but readily understood by their signs that they were hungry. We shared our supper with them, and they devoured their food with the voracity of famished wolves. Long after dark our guests, in single file, took their departure up the hill through the sage and we saw no more of them. If this had been a party of Blackfeet or Crow Indians, instead of these puny dwarfs, we might have considered ourselves in a trap; and yet, those war clubs, with the probability of a visit by a larger party some time during the night, was not very conducive to sound sleep. Two of our men, heavily armed, were on guard through the night, but nothing unusual occurred, though we did not feel fully assured of our safety until daylight the next morning, when we resumed our journey early without breakfast, and near noon found a little grass, but no water. Owing to the meager supply of water at our last night's camp, we were unable to fill our canteens in the morning, in consequence of which we suffered from thirst, as did also our animals; but awhile after dark we were much surprised at striking a small stream of running water and fairly good grass. Here we cooked and ate the last morsel of our food for supper, and, with the exception of one man on guard, we indulged in several hours of refreshing sleep.

We had intended to leave this camp soon after midnight on the morning of the 22d, but our extreme weariness after the forced marches, together with the horses showing signs of failure, held us to that running water till late in the morning. We never traveled faster than a slow walk, and in order to make forty miles a day it was necessary to be on the road fifteen or sixteen hours, which, with short rations for both man and beast, was extremely fatiguing, while we also suffered for the want of sleep.

We always had one man, and sometimes two, on watch while the others were sleeping, and this guard duty, which had to be so often repeated, together with our night marches and lack of food, was rapidly undermining our energy.

One of our mules becoming footsore, the pony was put under the saddle and "Old Mage" (the mule) was turned loose to follow. He was the finest looking mule in our outfit, yet, notwithstanding his glossy, mouse-colored coat and well-rounded form, he was possessed of a vixenish disposition and was a perfect tyrant among his fellows. While he and his master were the best of friends, he was always on kicking terms with everybody else. With his ears turned wrong side out and his teeth exposed to the weather, both man and beast acknowledged him the champion of the plains.

The terrible solitude which pervaded that desert region was very marked as we left camp that morning with empty stomachs. Our road led down the stream, and we were guessing and more than hoping that it would prove to be the Humboldt River. We traveled perhaps a little faster than usual, being anxious to overtake a wagon train or find something which could be converted into food. We were continually on the alert for jack-rabbits, having seen signs of them in the green spots along the road.

After seven or eight hours' travel we were still plodding down the stream, which was growing larger, and beginning to find small bottoms which were backed up by steep, rocky bluffs, giving the creek something of the appearance of a river, and we were almost convinced that it was the Humboldt.

With the exception of two or three short halts for our horses to crop a few blades of grass we kept steadily on our way, but found nothing to eat and could see no signs of a wagon train being near. The bluffs along the creek bottoms were more pronounced, and sharp spurs from them pushed down to the stream. In a ravine between two of these rocky points we fell in with a party of about twenty Indians, who seemed to be waiting by the roadside. Their nudity and long, matted hair, discordant voices, and hideous looking faces gave them the appearance of being a formidable crew. That they were bent on mischief there was no doubt, and, there being four or five of them to one of us, we watched them very closely, being prepared to meet any demonstration they might offer. The liberal supply of small arms which our friends had persuaded us to take along proved to be quite a comfort to us while parleying with these thievish Root Diggers.

As we approached them they commenced begging for something to eat. On finding that we had nothing for them, they began

123

bartering for our footsore mule, which was running loose without halter or bridle; but when they learned that cheap bows and war clubs were not legal tender for mules, and as we were about to move on, they concluded to take Old Mage without as much as saying "by your leave," and commenced driving him up the bed of a dry branch which made into the river at that point, and they succeeded in pulling and pushing him along for a short distance, when he concluded to join our company, and in freeing himself from his would-be captors six or eight Indians were knocked down and more or less hurt, while the others were so badly frightened that they made no further demonstration and we moved on unmolested. They were a pack of cowardly thieves and ought to have been shot on sight, but as Old Mage had fought his way out we left them and went our way, keeping a sharp lookout for robbers of the Humboldt at all points where they might be sheltered and take us by surprise. We traveled far into the night, as we wished to get some distance away from the party of Indians we had left behind, and also to increase our chances of overtaking a wagon train.

It was long after midnight when we halted on a very small stream of running water, which proved to be a tributary of the Humboldt, and here we tarried till morning. On viewing our surroundings at daylight, we were much disappointed at not finding traces of a wagon train having recently passed, and, as our only hope seemed to be in pushing ahead, we soon had our horses under the saddle; but before starting we discovered two ducks winging their way down the river bottom, and, as they were the first living thing that we had seen for a long time, we began to feel encouraged and were delighted at seeing them drop down in swampy-looking ground only two or three hundred yards from our camp. Fred and I, with our guns loaded for duck, started for the swamp, but we had proceeded only a short distance when a large jack-rabbit hopped out from among the willows, straightening himself up as if taking in the situation. Our anxiety and imagination, re-inforced by our empty stomachs, made that jack-rabbit look to be three or four feet high. Without the least hesitation, I think we made what modern hunters would call a pot-shot, but we got the rabbit. Returning to camp with our prize, we soon had choice cuts of rabbit cooking from the end of willow sticks, while Perkins produced about a tablespoonful of salt, which he had kept tied up in the corner of a very dirty handkerchief, and we enjoyed a glorious breakfast, with appetites sharpened by hard work and a long fast. Steve declared that "he who had never eaten broiled jack-rabbit, seasoned with salt, knew very little about good living."

The bottom on the west side of the river at this point was very wide, and the high, rocky bluffs, noticed the day before, seemed to have been transformed during our night march into mighty palisades, which were pushed back into a crescent shape, forming an amphitheatre of vast dimensions. There was no further question as to our being on the Humboldt.

It was arranged for Fred and I to canvass four or five miles of the river bottom for ducks, while the balance of the boys were to take our horses along and wait on the road for us to join them. There were many small ponds along the river bottom, on which ducks were sporting, but these little lakelets were all surrounded by a dense growth of brush and reeds, making it difficult to get within shooting distance. We found that ducks were not disposed to set themselves up as shining marks for "pot-hunters," and, not being expert wing-shots, we wasted some precious ammunition. We worked our way down the valley and in the swamps found

ducks quite numerous, and, forgetting everything foreign to the business in hand, enjoyed, for an hour or two, real oldtime sport.
We arrived at the five-mile limit with six
ducks and received the hearty congratula-
tions of our comrades. We were wet from
wading through the swamps and bespattered
with mud, but we cared little for that, for
in that desert country, where everything
seemed hungry, there was a satisfaction in
hustling for the crippled duck brought down
by a snap-shot, of which he who hunts for
pleasure alone knows nothing. After being
so pinched with hunger, the capture of half a
dozen small ducks made us feel that life was
yet worth living and that the world was
made to some purpose.

Chapter 10

WITH the ducks which we had taken
from the swamps hanging from our
saddles we pushed on down the valley
and entered a region of ashes, cinders, and
volcanic rocks, where there was not a trace
of vegetation. On our left, across the river,
was a low range of sterile mountains, which
formed the backing to the river bottom,
while on our right the solid rock wall noticed
in the morning continued with increasing
ruggedness.

About four o'clock p. m. we came to an old
camp ground where once had been a little
grass, but for us there was not a vestige left,
though a small patch of sage near by furnished fuel for cooking. There two of our
ducks, which had been plucked as we walked
along the road, were hurriedly cooked for

supper, when we again moved on, intending to travel until we found grass for our horses; but awhile after midnight, having found nothing but desert, we halted, tied our animals to rocks, posted a guard and indulged in a little sleep. At daylight there was nothing to do but take to the road again. We shortly came to a creek in which there was running water, and near by a camp ground which looked as though every company on the road had occupied it, for in the vicinity every blade of grass had been consumed. As our animals were suffering from hunger, we moved out towards the bluffs a mile or more, where was found good bunch-grass, and from boiled duck and duck soup we made an excellent breakfast.

Our camp being on a well worn Indian trail leading down through a break in the bluffs, with sheltering rocks all around us, we felt quite nervous and did not care to remain as marks for Indian arrows any longer than necessary to give our horses the benefit of the grass which they so much needed. We traveled rapidly down the river (if two and a half miles an hour can be called rapid traveling) and about the middle of the afternoon halted at a place which afforded a little grass, and there we finished the last of our ducks and started on again, but camped before dark in a grass plat where our horses grazed while we slept several hours, resuming our journey about midnight.

It seemed to be the plan of those Humboldt Indians to lie in wait at the camping places along the river for what they could beg or steal from travelers who occupied them. At one of those places, the next morning, we found a party of Indian beggars. That they were hungry there was no question, and, judging by their looks, they had always been hungry. Their nakedness, dwarfed bodies, and careworn expression excited our sympathy, while it was out of our power to offer them anything to appease their hunger.

At that point were found the irons of several wagons which had been left and the woodwork burned in making campfires. Much of the woodwork from abandoned wagons along the road was carried away by the Indians, but they seemed to care nothing for the iron, as we noticed quantities of it lying around in all the principal camping places. There were indications that this camp had been recently occupied, and we tried to learn something about it from the Indians, but in answer to our signs they only shook their heads and looked at each other with a puzzled expression. As we were about to leave, Perkins presented one of the Indians with an old pocketknife, but this only made them more persistent in their begging, for they followed us quite a distance, holding out their hands in a very beseeching manner.

Along in the afternoon we were somewhat excited by discovering canvas-topped wagons some distance down the river, and before night had overtaken them. They belonged to a company of men from Wisconsin, who had traveled all the way from that State with ox teams. In answer to our inquiries for provisions, we were told that their Captain, who was in advance looking for a camping place, was the only person authorized to sell or give away stores. We learned that they, like ourselves, after making a late start, had been detained by sickness, and, having taken but little game along the road, their supplies were about exhausted, while their oxen, in their poor and footsore condition, were barely able to travel. We shortly overtook the Captain, who was riding a very discouraged looking mule, and soon became acquainted, which was very natural in that lonesome and dreary country. The Captain invited us to spend the night in his camp, where he would have an ox killed and give us a portion of the meat, and we were more than glad to accept the proffered boon. A camp being selected and teams driven in, a poor, bony, footsore ox was singled out, shot, and dressed, and we were soon eating supper with appetites which made that dry beef better than any porterhouse steak ever eaten by an epicure in a civilized country. Of material from the head of that poor ox we made during the night a gallon of excellent soup, which we took along in our canteens, and from a portion of the skin made Old Mage a Mexican moccasin for his crippled foot. After taking supper and breakfast with the Captain, he gave us a few pounds of beef to take on the road. Being ready to start at daylight the next morning, we bade our kind friends adieu and resumed the journey, and never saw nor heard of any of them afterwards. After a long and tiresome day we camped about 10 o'clock p. m. where there was excellent grass for our horses.

About daybreak we were aroused by the guard, who had discovered campfires which seemed to be only a short distance away. Supposing that to mean a wagon train, we moved out without waiting for breakfast, as we desired to reach the camp before the train started on the road. We were surprised at finding all the wagons heading up the

stream, but soon learned that we had met a
party of Mormons on their way from California to the Mormon settlement near the
Great Salt Lake. They proved to be a mot-
ley crew. There were not only old men and
old women, young men and young women,
but a complete assortment of children of all
sizes and ages. From this people we obtained much valuable information in regard
to the road, camping places, and the distance to certain points. We also learned
that we were within twenty-five miles of the
sink of the Humboldt, and that we would be
under the necessity of making a long stretch
of sixty miles across a sandy plain which lay
between the sink of the Humboldt and the
next watering place. We were advised to
water our horses and fill our canteens from
the river at least ten miles above the sink,
and give that wonder of the world a wide
berth, as the water near the sink was so
strongly impregnated with alkali that it was
absolutely poisonous, while the grass in the
vicinity, owing to the overflow in the wet
season, was encrusted with potash and unfit
for grazing. The Mormons held out many
inducements for us to accompany them to
Salt Lake and spend the winter, but we declined with thanks. As they would follow our
trail as far as Bear River and were certain to

meet our company, it gave us an opportunity of notifying them as to our progress and prospects. We subsequently learned that our message was properly delivered and that the Mormons sold our company four head of beef cattle, though at many times their actual value. Being about to resume the journey, our Mormon friends presented us with four or five pounds of flour, a pint of rice, and a very small quantity of salt. In addition to a drove of cattle which they were taking with them, their wagons were heavily loaded with goods and provisions, but they flatly refused to sell us supplies at any price.

In considering the enfeebled condition of ourselves and animals at that time, we had some misgivings as to our ability to make a continuous march of sixty miles across a hot, sandy region without water or grass, though a very tempting and encouraging feature of the undertaking was the promise of excellent grass and water after crossing the sand plain, or, as the Mormons called it, the Great American Desert. In order to spare our animals we walked many miles every day, but found it very fatiguing, which, together with the loss of sleep and insufficient food, seemed to be gradually wearing us out, while our riding animals were growing poor and liable to fail us at any time.

We were almost afraid to ride for fear of falling from the saddle while sleeping. David, one of our party, who, for the want of proper food, had become prostrated, was continually growing weaker, and, at that time, unable to mount his horse without help.

Though the future looked gloomy and uncertain, yet knowing that the lives of ourselves and of our friends in the rear depended, to a great extent, on the accomplishment of our object, we banished all doubts of final success and plodded along, consoling ourselves with the knowledge that every mile gained brought us nearer our journey's end.

We arrived at the last camping place on the Humboldt by three o'clock p. m., and after watering our horses and filling our canteens we moved out about a mile towards the bluffs, where we found good grass and managed, by burning dry weeds, to cook an allowance of food to last us across the desert.

Although we were anxious as to the result of the next two or three days' travel, yet we welcomed the prospect of leaving the Humboldt and its dreary valley behind.

The reader should not imagine the Humboldt to be a rapid mountain stream, with its cool and limpid waters rushing down the rocks of steep inclines, with here and there

135

beautiful cascades and shady pools under mountain evergreens, where the sun never intrudes and where the speckled trout loves to sport. While the water of such a stream is fit for the gods, that of the Humboldt is not good for man nor beast. With the exception of a short distance near its source, it has the least perceptible current. There is not a fish nor any other living thing to be found in its waters, and there is not timber enough in three hundred miles of its desolate valley to make a snuff-box, or sufficient vegetation along its banks to shade a rabbit, while its waters contain the alkali to make soap for a nation, and, after winding its sluggish way through a desert within a desert, it sinks, disappears, and leaves inquisitive man to ask how, why, when and where?

On August 26th, after watering our horses, filling the canteens and also our coffeepot, which was carried by turns, we were off at break of day, and by noon were fairly launched upon a vast sea of mingled ashes and sand, which was so compact that our animals, in traveling over it, rarely left a footprint, while the burning rays of the sun reflected from the smooth surface made the heat almost unbearable. We were crossing the bed of an ancient lake which seemed to the eye to be absolutely level. It was seventy miles long and sixty miles wide, and nowhere on its surface was seen a trace of vegetable or animal life. In some long past age this lake received the waters of the Humboldt, Carson, and Walker rivers, but by some unaccountable change of levels the rivers found other outlets, and this arid waste added another mystery to that mysterious region.

On arriving at the sink of the Humboldt, a great disappointment awaited us. We had known nothing of the nature of that great wonder except what we had been told by those who knew no more about it than ourselves. In place of a great rent in the earth, into which the waters of the river plunged with a terrible roar (as pictured in our imagination), there was found a mud lake ten miles long and four or five miles wide, a veritable sea of slime, a "slough of despond," an ocean of ooze, a bottomless bed of alkaline poison, which emitted a nauseous odor and presented the appearance of utter desolation. The croaking of frogs would have been a redeeming feature of the place, but no living thing disturbed the silence and solitude of the lonely region. There were mysteries and wonders hovering over and around the sink of the Humboldt, but there was neither beauty nor grandeur in connection with it, for a more dreary or desolate spot could not be found on the face of the earth.

For several miles around the lake there was a low, sandy plain, which was nearly on a level with the lake itself and subject to overflow during the wet season, as evidenced by the large deposits of crystallized potash left on the surface after the water subsided.

The valley of the Humboldt, lying between two mountain ranges, was extremely hot during the summer, and, there being no rainfall in that country for a period of eight months of the year, the question arose in our minds whether absorption and evaporation might not solve the mystery of the sinking of the Humboldt.

Sometime after midnight we discovered a bright fire in the direction we were traveling, and, as it appeared to be a great way off, we took it for granted that it was on Carson River, just beyond the desert. We were highly elated at the prospect of shaking off this desert so early, and to relieve our thirst we drew on our canteens quite freely, which was afterwards regretted.

It was daylight when we arrived at the fire, where we found several wagons but no animals of any description, while the same trackless waste reached out in all directions. The reader can imagine how keen was our disappointment when a solitary man, who had charge of the camp, informed us that we were yet twenty miles from water. We had traveled twenty-four hours without a halt, and, in order to spare our animals, the most of the way had been made on foot, and, being extremely hungry, thirsty, and weary, we were sorely disappointed. The wagons belonged to a company from Missouri, who, after thirty hours' travel from the Humboldt, found their oxen so exhausted as to be unable to take the wagons through, and, in order to save them, they were unyoked and driven to the river, where they were being herded until sufficiently recruited to be taken back for the wagons.

Perkins was selected to solicit this lone man for supplies, and for a bright five-dollar gold piece he secured about four quarts of flour, a pint of rice, and a pinch or two of salt. In justice to the many kind persons who furnished the supplies which kept us from starving by the wayside, I will state that the man who had charge of those wagons was the only person who accepted money for provisions. We never passed a single company without being made welcome to such supplies as could be spared from their scanty stores, which speaks well for the noble, free-hearted souls that crossed the plains in forty-nine. Halting at this point but a few minutes, we hurried on, and after a continuous march of thirty-four hours, during which time we suffered with hunger, thirst, and heat, we arrived at the river about 3 o'clock p. m. On the last twenty miles of our march we passed the skeletons of many animals which had perished before they could reach the water. Oxen died with their yokes still on them, while horses and mules lay dead in their harness, and property of all kinds, even bedding, was scattered along the road. Wagons, from which their canvas tops had not been removed, were shrinking in the hot sun, with the tires ready to fall from their wheels. Oxen, after making a desperate fight for their lives, perished within a mile of the river, while everything along the road gave evidence of there having been terrible suffering by both man and beast.

Dinner being disposed of, we began to look around to see what we could find for our horses, but it seemed as though all travelers who had crossed the desert camped down as soon as they struck the river, and consequently there was not a particle of grass anywhere in the vicinity; and, as our animals were starving, we moved up the river two or three miles, where we forded the stream and on a rich bottom, among the tussock willows, there was splendid grazing.

It fell to my lot to guard the camp till midnight, and, without loss of time the other boys threw themselves under their blankets and were asleep in a trice. With a blanket over my shoulders, fastened at the throat with a wooden pin and with two revolvers and my gun ready for immediate use, I was equipped for several hours of lonely and weary watch. There was yet an hour of daylight, and in my exhausted condition I could see no necessity of walking a regular beat (as was the rule) before sundown, at least, and in order to take a few minutes' rest I seated myself on the ground with my gun lying across my lap, while my back was supported by a thick cluster of willows. The next morning, just as the sun was showing his face over the tops of the mountains which lay to the east, I awoke with a start. I was not long in mastering the situation. I had slept all night and the other boys were still sleeping, while our mules and horses, which were near by, seemed oblivious to everything on earth.

Following up Carson River, we encamped, a while after dark on August 31st, near the point where the river came rushing through one of the highest ridges in the Sierra

Nevada mountains, by the way of Echo Canyon.[38]

The class in geology will please stand up and tell us how many thousands of years it has taken this little river to cut its way to a depth of three thousand feet for a distance of seven miles through this noble mountain, and also tell us how many millions of tons of earth and eroded rock have been carried away by the waters of this insignificant stream.

As our road lay through the canyon, we entered it early in the morning, and, after crossing the river seventeen times in traveling six miles, we arrived about noon at a point near the head of the canyon, where the immense rocks which had fallen from above made it almost impossible to get wagons through. Here we found two young men who hailed from Missouri, and who had left

[38] Shaw's party crossed the Sierras by way of Carson Pass, the route taken by Fremont on his visit to California in the winter of 1843-44. From Carson Pass, Shaw and his companions made their way, by a route difficult to determine with certainty to and down Webber Creek, and so on to Sacramento. U.S. Highway 50 from Carson City to Sacramento parallels this route, although somewhat farther north in its eastern portion, where it passes the southern end of Lake Tahoe, and along the South Fork of the American River. At Placerville, which Shaw does not mention, U.S. 50 approaches within a couple of miles the site of Weberville, which Shaw presently describes.

home with two yoke of small oxen and an old wagon which was quite unfit for such a journey, as it broke down before they got through the Rocky Mountains; but, using the larger wheels of the wagon, they fitted up a cart which served them until they struck the mass of rocks at that point, where it was completely wrecked. Without hesitating a moment, they commenced packing their oxen with their effects and were soon ready for the road again. For protection, these boys had kept along with a large company of wagoners, and were then hurrying to overtake them. In answer to our inquiries for supplies, they offered to share with us a very meager store, but, as our larder was good for another meal, we declined the generous gift.

We passed from the canyon into a narrow valley between two high, parallel ranges of mountains. Our animals having had but little to eat for over thirty hours, we moved up the valley off the road, and among the immense rocks, which in past ages had rolled down the steep mountainside, they found a scanty supply of grass, while we, under a large, scrubby cedar, whose low, drooping branches formed a perfect shade, rested for a couple of hours. We encamped at night close by a company of wagoners, who gave us a few pounds of foot-sore beef.

Our road on September 2d led south down the valley between the high ridges, but along in the afternoon it turned abruptly to the right, and through a depression in the ridge, by what old mountaineers would call an easy trail, we crossed the second barrier and camped for the night on the border of a small lake of pure water, at the base of the highest and last mountain to be crossed, for beyond the summit lay the promised land. As it was very cold and fuel being abundant, we kept a rousing fire through the night, for our blankets afforded but little protection from the extreme cold of that high altitude, where water froze every night.

Chapter 11

ABOUT noon on September 3rd, after a climb of over six hours, we arrived at the summit of the pass over the highest range of the Sierra Nevada Mountains. On reaching the summit of that vast pile, and being surrounded by the solitude and silence peculiar to high altitudes, we stood gazing down into the beautiful Sacramento Valley, where we hoped to end our journey and our sufferings. For some little time not a word was spoken, and I imagine we all felt as one coming in sight of home after a long absence and a perilous journey. This pass, which is ten thousand and five hundred feet above sea level, is the highest point ever reached by any wagon road in our country, and, though scaling the mountain with wagons was a difficult task, yet a limited number of them were taken across and, in a worn and battered condition, sent down into the mines, where they were looked

145

upon by Cape Horners as relics of civilization.

Of the thousands of wagons which left the frontier the wreckage of most of them might have been found in the camping places between the Platte River and the foot of this mountain. After a short halt, in order to enjoy the grandeur and beauty of our surroundings, we moved rapidly down towards the Sacramento, and at night slept under the red woods.

The next morning, after cooking and eating the last of our food for breakfast, we were off early, for we expected to reach the mining camps sometime during the day. Our road led down steep slopes among the scattering live-oaks and tall pines. About sundown we passed a number of well-constructed brush huts, and there were indications of them having been recently occupied; but, there being no water or grass in the vicinity, we moved on, hoping to find something to appease our extreme hunger, and, two hours after dark, having found nothing for ourselves or animals, we came to a grove of small birch saplings on the gentle slope of a hill, and there, with our horses tied to the trees, we encamped for the night.

Early next morning we discovered a man at work in a ravine at the foot of the hill on which we had spent the night, and learned from him that we were close to Webber Creek mines, and that a short distance away we should find a wagon store, where we could buy supplies of all kinds. With our coffee-pot and canteens we visited the peddler's wagon, and from stores there purchased we prepared an excellent breakfast, and for the time being our craving for molasses, vinegar, and salt was fully appeased. The amount of food consumed at that breakfast seemed to be measured more by the capacity of our stomachs than by our appetites, for, after having been so long pinched with hunger, the appetite never seemed satisfied.

There being no grass in the vicinity of our camp, it was arranged for Steve and me to take the animals a mile or two down the valley, and, by agreement, Steve was to lead one of the mules while I drove the others after him. As we were ready to set out, Steve, noticing three flapjacks which had been left from breakfast, remarked that, as they were seasoned with salt and swimming in molasses, he didn't propose to get two miles from them, and seizing them he started, carrying the plate in one hand and leading a mule with the other. After fifteen minutes' travel, Steve called me to come and help him, as he was having trouble with the flap-

jacks. On joining him I found that the hot
sun to which the molasses had been exposed
caused it to overflow the plate, and Steve,
in order to protect his clothing, was holding
it at arm's length, with the molasses trickling
down between his fingers, while he was
lamenting over the loss of so much sweet-
ness. Seating ourselves on a rock, we took
good care that there should be no further
waste of ready-made luxuries, leaving the
empty plate on the rock.

A temporary shelter was constructed for
David, one of our party, as it was arranged
for him to remain at that place until our return, in order to recruit his health, as he was
still suffering from the effects of improper
food. We spent the afternoon viewing Webber town and among the miners along the
creek. The town at that early day consisted
of about a dozen small tents and several
covered wagons, one of which was known as
"The Store," while quite a large log house
was being constructed for a hotel.[39] The

[39] "Webber town," commonly called Weberville,
was named for Captain Charles M. Weber, who in 1848,
in cooperation with Indian Chief José Jesús began mining operations on the site, about two miles south of
Placerville. Weber opened a store, whose goods he
exchanged for the gold mined by Jesús and his twenty-
five followers. The red men as yet had slight knowledge
of money values, and Weber utilized his profits to

rainy season not yet having set in, many of the miners were cooking and eating in the open air, while their only shelter for the night were very rudely constructed brush huts. We formed the acquaintance of two young men (late arrivals) who were partners in mining. The only washer they were as yet able to procure was a four-quart tin pan, with which one of them separated the gold from the dirt, while the other, with a very small pick which seemed admirably adapted to the work, was supplying the pan with a limited quantity of pay dirt from pockets and crevices among the rocks; but with that primitive outfit they claimed to be making twenty dollars each per day.

We noticed that only a small amount of dirt could be taken from the bar on which

---

found the town of Tuleburg, which he presently renamed Stockton. To Weberville late this same season of 1849 came a forlorn family of tenderfeet, Mr. and Mrs. Josiah Royce. Mrs. Royce was a remarkable woman and her son Josiah, born in 1856, became the noted Harvard University philosopher of the following generation. Mrs. Royce's narrative was utilized by her son in writing his *California from the Conquest in 1846 to the Second Vigilance Committee in San Francisco, A Study of American Character* (Boston, 1886). Mrs. Royce's own story was subsequently published in 1932, entitled *Frontier Lady; Recollections of the Gold Rush and Early California.*

these men were working, but later we learned
that placer diggings, creek and river bars
were composed of about four parts of rock
and one of pay dirt, and to extract it from
among the compact mass of water-worn,
globular-shaped rocks of all sizes required
patience, time, and labor. The most of the
miners were using pans ten to fifteen inches
in diameter, and they reported their profits
at ten to fifty cents to the pan.

The rocker, which in shape and size resembled the old-fashioned infant's cradle, was
just being introduced and was a great improvement over the pan. It was rather a
plain affair and easily made, though it was
worth at that time from forty to fifty dollars.
A carpenter, with good tools and suitable
lumber at hand, could make two or three of
them in a day; but when we considered the
fact that wages were from twelve to twenty
dollars per day, and that the lumber, after
being rived from red-wood logs with much
labor, had to be shaved and dressed with such
tools as could be had in the mines, while a
piece of sheet iron sixteen inches square
required for each rocker, was ready sale at
five dollars, the price seemed quite reasonable. Another machine, called the "long
tom," was worked by some of the miners,
but they soon dropped out of use, as they

proved to be poor separators, leaving their tailings very rich.

The principal food of the miners at that time consisted of stewed beans and flapjacks, and they were generally served twenty-one times a week, though the latter occasionally gave place to flour dumplings boiled in clear water and eaten with molasses, the whole forming the most indigestible combination that could well be imagined; consequently many a miner, after a brief stay, left California for his home with more dyspepsia than gold. Those who were tinctured with scurvy, resulting from their long journey across the plains or a voyage around Cape Horn, by the advice of physicians were adding to their bill of fare such luxuries as onions at two dollars per pound and vinegar at a dollar a pint. Pepsin, pills, and epsom salts were in active demand and sold at fabulous prices.

We left that pleasant camp early on the morning of September 6th for Sutter's Fort, or, as it is now called, Sacramento City, for supplies to take back to our company, having learned that they could not be obtained at any nearer point.

Two days' march from Webber Creek brought us to a point on the American River, three miles from Sacramento City. We met a great many Cape Horners on their way to

the mines. The most of them were on foot
and carrying their camping outfit on their
backs. As they had been from four to six
months on shipboard, with very limited
space in which to exercise, they found walking and carrying a pack extremely fatiguing;
but, as they were puffed up with prospective
wealth, they were sure to overcome all difficulties.

Early next morning we moved down to the
city, where we purchased and packed our
animals with fourteen hundred pounds of
supplies, and soon after dark were back in
the camp we had occupied the night before.
Old Mage was packed with three hundred
pounds of barley, which was fed to our animals on the return trip. Having been very
busy preparing our packs, it was past one
o'clock p.m. before we could leave the work
for dinner, though our stomachs had notified
us of our hunger for an hour or two.

We were directed to what was said to be
the best "feeding place" in the city. Over
the main entrance was painted on white canvas, in large letters, "City Hotel." On in-
quiring the price of meals, the landlord informed us that the regular rate was five dollars, but remarked that "as there were four
of us and it being past the dinner hour, he
would feed our party for an ounce. An

ounce of gold-dust in California at that time was rated equal to sixteen dollars in coin, though, if reasonably clean, its intrinsic value was more than eighteen dollars. There was no paper money in circulation, and the coin of the country was nearly all absorbed by gamblers who found it best adapted to their business.

Though gold dust was about the only circulating medium, yet he who possessed it could buy anything from a fifty-cent cigar to a ten-thousand-dollar corner lot in any of the prospective capitals of California.

While dinner was being prepared we improved the opportunity in examining the construction of the hotel building, which we estimated to be thirty feet long and about twelve feet wide. Pine strips, one by three inches, nailed together, formed the frame, and it was covered with the cheapest of calico. Eighteen or twenty feet of the front end was used as a dining-room, while the balance was curtained off for a kitchen. This being the first roof under which we had eaten for several months, we enjoyed the novelty of the situation. The proprietor apologized for the close quarters in which he was doing business, and informed us that previous to leaving New York he had shipped a building ("knocked down") around Cape Horn, for a hotel, but up to that time it had not arrived. Our dinner consisted of navy bread, stewed beans, fresh salmon, raw onions, molasses, boiled potatoes, river water, and tea. I may here remark that a year later, at the City Hotel (a large frame building), excellent meals were furnished for one dollar. In commenting on our dinner, Steve remarked that "though the price seemed pretty steep, yet he was doubtful whether the landlord realized any net profit from our patronage."

Risking my reputation for veracity, I will name the prices which we paid for supplies: Flour, $18 per hundred; rice, 45c per pound; sugar, 30c; potatoes, 20c; onions, $1; beans, 23c; tea, $3.50; barley, 16c; cooking soda, $1; salt, 22c; black molasses, $3.50 per gallon; vinegar, which was in active demand as a remedy for scurvy, was selling at $1.25 per quart. Round-pointed shovels sold at $20 each; square-pointed shovels, $1.50; miners' picks, $16 each; Cape Horn picks (not adapted to mining), $1. Carpenters were being offered $16 to $25 per day to work at their trade, and common laborers were in demand at $200 per month, but they all seemed to think that princely fortunes were awaiting them in the mines and declined working for wages. Men with teams were asking $30 to

$40 per day for hauling goods to the mines, and they were well patronized.

We were deeply interested in the make-up of Sacramento City, which, in a year after our visit, became the capital of the State of California. There was not a complete frame building in the place at that time, though there were a number in course of construction, but there were tents and canvas houses of all sorts and sizes. They were occupied as stores, hotels, boarding houses, gambling and drinking saloons. Gamblers were plying their vocation with a persistency worthy of a better cause, and where shelter was not to be had games were being worked in the open air.

We noticed a Mexican lad exhibiting his superior horsemanship and skill in throwing the lasso. He had a small dog, which probably had been trained for the business, for the dog and horse seemed to understand each other. While both were at their best speed, the boy never failed to capture the dog by the neck with the lasso. The rider also plucked his hat from the ground while his pony was on a dead run. He invited any of the bystanders to place a coin on his handkerchief which he had spread on the ground, and, without his pony slacking speed in the least, he would secure the coin. This at the present time might be considered a very tame affair, but for us, who knew nothing of horsemanship except what we had experienced in crossing the plains, it was quite interesting.

A number of ships which had fought their way around Cape Horn were lying at anchor in the Sacramento and discharging their cargoes on the bank of the river. Hundreds of men who had just arrived in the country and were preparing to go to the mines were loading wagons and packing broken-down horses and mules with their winter stores.

A crowd of men had gathered around a large box, on which stood a young man expatiating on the good qualities of the ship *Strafford*, which lay at anchor in the stream, with an auctioneer's flag displayed from her main yard. The young man, who seemed to be a novice in the business, was about to sell the ship at auction to the highest bidder, and finally succeeded in knocking her off for eight hundred dollars. She probably cost not less than six thousand. Nearly all of the Cape Horn companies disbanded on arriving at their destination, and many of their ships were sold for almost nothing, while not a few were left at anchor in the harbor of San Francisco, where they became worm-eaten and foul with barnacles and were finally condemned by inspectors as being unseaworthy.

Three days of hard work in walking and driving loaded mules brought us back to Webber Creek, where we found David much improved in health and ready to help us climb the Sierra Nevada on the return to our company. We slowly worked our way up the steep mountain, and about noon on the fifth day from Webber Creek we partook of a cold lunch on the very summit of the highest ridge of the Sierras, and at the same time enjoyed the best bird's-eye view of grand mountain scenery to be had anywhere in this country. We were in excellent spirits, our voracious appetites having surrendered to full and wholesome rations, and we were in condition to enjoy the immensity of the surroundings. Away to the north could be seen the snow-capped summit of conical peaks, while to the south immense ridges, with their canyons, gorges, and lakelets, continued until lost to view in the distance.[40] To the west a dense haze obstructed the vision, and it looked as though one might step off into space, while the east revealed to our gaze a

[40] From this, or another near-by peak, Fremont in 1844 had gazed northward upon an extensive mountain lake, world-famous today as Lake Tahoe. Although some of Shaw's superlatives may perhaps be questioned, his enthusiasm for the mountain scenery he describes is amply justified.

continuous mass of rocks, cliffs and mountains which seemed to be thrown together in utter confusion.

Here, where ox teams drew wagons over the crest, we were more than five thousand feet higher than the crater of Mt. Vesuvius, and nearly as high as the summit of Mt. Etna, while the snow-crowned peaks of this immense pile still reached heavenward.

Let him visit the mountains of Europe who will, and climb the Alps, and explore the Apennines, but here within our own boundaries he may find a greater than the Alps, while the Apennines are as pigmies compared to this majestic upheaval. Nowhere in all Europe will our tourist find a mightier range of grand old mountains, with loftier peaks or deeper canyons. Nowhere will he find more magnificent rocks, beautiful natural parks, or verdant vales. Nowhere will he find more sublime waterfalls or finer mountain lakes. Nowhere in Europe will he find mammoth trees three hundred feet high, surrounded by precipitous rocks reaching three thousand feet above them. Nowhere will he find sunnier skies, or a greater wealth of primitive plants mantled in gorgeous bloom. Nowhere in Europe will he find the equal of our geysers, hot and boiling springs, mud lakes, great deserts, natural meadows and lost rivers.

We were all the afternoon working our way down the eastern slope of the mountain, camping at night for the second time on the border of the little lake previously mentioned, where a good fire through the night hardly kept us from suffering with cold. During the night ice again formed on the surface of the lake and the morning was chilly, with heavy frost.

We continued our return journey as fast as our heavily laden animals could be forced along, and on September 20th about an hour after dark at a point on Carson River, within a few rods of where we had enjoyed the best night's sleep of our lives, we were hailed by a familiar voice, and there, encamped among the tussock willows, we found our starving company. The joy which followed the meeting may be imagined, but never described.

Index

Index

Index

Index

GADSDEN Purchase, 6.

Gage, Joseph B., Indians frighten, 50.

Gaines, Ruth, edits *Gold Rush*, xl.

Gold, discovered, xix-xx, 9; mining operations described, 149-51. See also Gold-seekers.

Gold-seekers, characterized, xxiii; anticipations, xxiv-xxvi; rush to California, xxvii-xxx, 9-11; discard property, xxvi-xxx, 53, 55-56, 116; routes to California, xx-xxiii, 14-15; encounters with Indians, 30-34, 47-50, 75-77, 85-99, 119-21; in storms, 34-35, 62-64; wash clothes, 105-106; encounter emigrants, 117-18, 131-32, 138-39; hospitality, 139-40, 142-43.

Goose Creek, gold-seekers camp, 109-11.

Granite State and California Mining and Trading Company, members accompany Mount Washington Mining Company, xl, 11, 18. See also Kimball Webster.

Greenwood, Caleb, opens Cut-Off, 58.

Greenwood Cut-Off. See Sublette Cut-Off.

Great American Desert, 134.

Great Basin, explored, 6-7; gold-seekers traverse, 110-41, 159.

Great Bend, of Humboldt River, route via, xxiii.

Great Salt Lake, Stansbury survey, xxvi-xxvii.

HASKINS, C. W., narrative cited, xxiv, 11.

Hastings, Lansford P., advice, xxxii.

Haynes, Dr. J. N., joins gold-seekers, 11-12; medical service, 19, 23-24, 50, 80, 82; activities, 27, 44-46, 84, 86, 111.

Hinckley, D. W., death, 23-24.

Horses, gold-seekers use, xxxi-xxxiv, 12; die, xxix, 140; purchased, 18; stolen, 22; hunt buffaloes, 52-53; advance party selects, 112-13; give out, 121. See also Mules and Oxen.

Hot Springs, 116-17.

Hudspeth's (Emigrants') Cut-Off, route via, xxii-xxiii.

Index

166

Index

Index

Index

Index